Praise for *Blend. Science with Sp.*

In *Blending Science with Spices* registered dietitian, Gita Patel, takes us on a spectacular culinary journey through western India providing the reader with an array of nutritious and light Gujarati-style dishes. For each recipe, we are treated to visually exquisite, delightfully delicious, quick and easy-to-make fare. Gita serves up healthy and superbly flavorful Gujarati delights like eggplant with onions and tomatoes–each recipe with full nutrition information and a little nutrition science to highlight the ingredients. *Blending Science with Spices* is the perfect cookbook for healthy eaters who want to eat simple and oh so flavorful plant-based meals.

– *Janet Bond Brill, PhD, RD*
Nutritionist and author

In *Blending Science with Spices*, author Gita Patel, Registered Dietitian and Certified Diabetes Educator, has woven healthy, nutritious recipes with an evidence-based rationale for the science of nutrition to substantiate each and every recipe.

The recipes are easy to prepare, they are plant based from the state of Gujarat in India; with detailed nutrient information. They are special as they are traditional, family recipes; yet easy to prepare and something for every palate.

This cookbook is a recommended addition to one's cookbook collection.

– *Karmeen Kulkarni, MS, RD, BC-ADM, CDE*
Author/Nutrition Consultant/Speaker

Tired and wrung out from work, I would start munching crackers and anything else easy to fill up on... not healthy!

Gita has changed all that! My kitchen is now stocked with healthy food I can quickly grab and turn into nutritious suppers for my family in minutes! The calories are low; we enjoy the taste; and we feel very pleasantly full! We used to keep "grazing" all evening, never satisfied. No more!

– *Jeanne Childs, Patient*

Informative and uplifting reading style! This practical vegetarian cookbook will transform your kitchen into an instant take-out place for healthy food. The recipes will make you fall in love with preparing healthy vegetarian entrees and side dishes with great ease. Gita Patel has skillfully unfolded the mysteries of Indian vegetarian cooking and the use of Indian spices.

– Geeta Sikand, MA, RD, FADA, CDE, CLS
Consultant Dietitian/Author/Speaker
Associate Clinical Professor of Medicine: Cardiology
University of California Irvine College of Medicine

In *Blending Science with Spices*, Gita Patel MS, RD, CDE has skillfully combined components of the plant kingdom to provide delicious and easy to prepare vegetarian food. Her recipes from Gujarat add to the repertoire of world cuisines that can help promote sustainable healthful lifestyles. In addition the nutrient values of each recipe will help make informed choices in meal preparation.

– Wahida Karmally, DrPH,RD,CDE,CLS,FNLA
Associate Research Scientist, Lecturer in Dentistry
Director of Nutrition, Irving Institute for Clinical and Translational Research
Columbia University

Feeding Health™

Blending Science with Spices

Tasty Recipes & Nutrition Tips for Healthy Living

Vegetarian ▪ Gluten Free ▪ Indian

BY

Gita Patel, MS RD CDE LD

www.FeedingHealth.com

ISBN: 978-0-9835258-0-6
First Edition: July 2011

To order a copy of this book, please visit:
www.FeedingHealth.com

Photography by Jane Bedford, Etna, NH
Cover and Book Design by Lufkin Graphic Designs, Norwich, VT

Disclaimer: This book is intended as a reference volume only, not as a medical manual.
The information given here is designed to help you make informed decisions about your
health. It is not intended as a substitute for any treatment that may have been prescribed
by your doctor. Please consult your health professional for medical advice. Although
every effort has been made to provide accurate and up-to-date information, this book
cannot guarantee to be free of factual error. The author shall have no liability of any kind
for damages of any nature howsoever caused and will not accept any responsibility for
any errors, omissions or misstatements that may exist within this publication.

Printed in USA

Published by
Gita Patel
Feeding Health™
7 Partridge Road
Etna, NH 03750

www.FeedingHealth.com

Contents

Foreword

In this day of endless "diet" and "eat right" books exhorting us all to better nutritional health, Gita Patel's simple approach to cooking and consuming whole vegetables and grains is most welcome. Some 25 years ago I had the enormous good fortune to be a student in several Indian cooking classes taught by Ms. Patel, where I became acquainted with the charms of Gujarati cooking, from raita and rice pilafs to casseroles and parathas, naan, chapattis and everything in between. Along the way I learned a good deal about nutrition – all vegetarian – and the use of low or no-fat ingredients, timesavers in the kitchen, and the exotic flavors of Indian cuisine.

For Gita Patel not only taught us the recipes, but she showed us how to make our own exquisite yogurt at home (without a fancy electric yogurt maker); how to keep tastes like fresh gingerroot, garlic, and jalapeno peppers at the ready in the freezer; how to cook in quantity and to save at least half in the freezer for future meals. And she demonstrated, almost intuitively, how to mix grains, legumes, and vegetables to get the most nutritious result, and how to use vegetables and spices to add color and zest to every dish. To this day I keep food-processed garlic, ginger root, and jalapenos in jars or plastic bags in the freezer, ready to use at a moment's notice in any dish – Asian, Indian or otherwise.

For our recent kitchen upgrade, I designed an entire 12 x 12 inch spice drawer right next to the stove, for all the Indian spices I needed: cumin, turmeric, cardamom, black pepper seeds, whole cloves, cinnamon sticks, hing, and many others. I can look at any Indian recipe and easily modify it by reducing the fat and salt, adding more flavors, and using colorful vegetables instead of meats. The Indian cooking classes opened a world of flavors and nutrition that I had never known before.

Ms Patel's book is most welcome in this day of over nutrition, obesity, high fat foods, over salting, risks for diabetes mellitus, and gluten-laden foods that most of us are constantly exposed to. To prepare foods from the garden or the local farmer's market, along with carefully chosen grains and legumes and spices, all for a fraction of the fat content and the cost of restaurant food (or "fast" food), is a cook's dream. Indian vegetarian cuisine, made as simple or complex as desired, with few or many spices, provides a roadmap to health through eating. With fresh local ingredients and a well-stocked kitchen, one can prepare a wonderful, healthy meal in 30 minutes – talk about "fast"! And it is no exaggeration that for only a few dollars, using local or garden vegetables and items stocked in my kitchen, I can prepare a six-dish vegetarian Indian meal for friends. Best of all, this meal will contain essentially no trans-fat or cholesterol.

Ms Patel's book will guide you in how to cook and eat well – to eat for health – and will remind you of the science behind good eating. Let it open for you the same doors to a new world of taste and health as it did for my family and me.

Carole A. Stashwick, MD, PhD
Dept of Pediatrics
Dartmouth Medical School

Acknowledgments

No nutrition cookbook trying to merge the East with the West in light of our contemporary lifestyles is created alone. It would have been impossible for me to complete this book without the support and guidance of my friends, colleagues and family. This project has been a team effort and I am very thankful for their help. I am deeply grateful for the countless hours of help, encouragement, guidance, editing and support from my friends:

Diane Russell, Jane Bedford, Jeanne Childs, Linda Bedford and Sandra Johnson; Dr Carole Stashwick for writing the forward; colleagues Janine Higgins, PhD and Dr. Thomas M. Wnorowski for their contributions; colleagues Aarti Batavia, Geeta Sikand, Sarah Ellis and Susan Linke for their editing and constructive feedback; book designer Douglas Lufkin; my family – Dipak, Kamini and Sanjay; my children – Krupa, Ram, Anjali, and Rob; Dana Angelo White, MS, RD who did the recipe analysis and editor Shelby Grantham. I am also grateful to my patients, who have been waiting a long time for this book.

Dedication

I dedicate this book to my mother, Dayalaxmi, who kindled my passion to understand how food affects the body. She passed away last year at the age of 98. She grew up on a village farm in Karakhadi, in Gujarat, India. In my mother's day, Karakhadi had neither a doctor nor a hospital and vitamins and supplements were unheard of. Since the whole village relied on foods to maintain health my mother's medicine came solely from the kitchen.

She taught herself Ayurveda, an ancient philosophy and life science including diet, healing, and health maintenance. In Ayurveda, medicine and diet are complementary and inclusive, and the science is founded on the powerful effect that food has on physical health, mental clarity and spiritual progress.

I questioned her beliefs, and later studied the effects of foods on the body so that I could challenge her faith in food as medicine. Ironically, my study led me to share this faith in the Ayurvedic principles, and to feel profoundly grateful for the inspiration my mother had given me.

How This Book Came About

As a Registered Dietitian and Certified Diabetes Educator, I see patients with a wide range of chronic conditions, all of which can respond to medical nutrition therapy: diabetes, heart disease, high cholesterol, high blood pressure, weight management, cancer, women's conditions, food sensitivities, food allergies and celiac disease (p.146).

My patients tell me the fast pace of today's "developed" world makes it hard to eat well. Who has the time to prepare meals from scratch, let alone create healthful, varied and appetizing menus? My patients say over and over again that all the knowledge in the world about nutrition does no good if it cannot be implemented easily.

The purpose of this book is to show how to choose health, understand nutrition science, and easily put the information to use right in your own kitchen. When you get home from work at 5:30 pm and the whole family is tired and hungry, you want to reach for whatever is "quick and easy." I will show you how to make your kitchen into an "instant take-out" hub. Your freezer and pantry will be stocked with wonderfully healthy grains, beans, hummus, pesto and one-dish meals, ready to thaw and serve! At last you will have the knowledge and ability to put "Feeding Health" into action.

I also want to share with you my approach to healthful cooking which combines modern nutritional science with my traditional vegetarian Indian heritage. When we became ill where I grew up in India, the medicine came from our kitchen. Our cough syrup, for instance, was a liquid made of ½ teaspoon each of turmeric and clarified butter with a pinch of salt in two ounces of warm milk, taken just before bed. We now know that turmeric contains antioxidant and anti-inflammatory curcumin, an excellent treatment for a sore throat. My mother treated our stomach ailments with herbs and spices mixed with a little asafetida and fresh limejuice.

For a cold, cough or sore throat, we were given Indian gooseberries (amla fruit) to suck, plus turmeric or other herbal-spice preparations high in vitamin C and antioxidants. How vividly I remember our daily dose of jeevan! Jeevan, which means "life," is a paste made from amla fruit mixed with many herbs and spices. The taste was pleasant and we didn't mind a spoonful every morning to keep our immune systems healthy.

Thus I learned early in life how to keep my immune system healthy. My goal in this book is to help all of you, my readers, improve the quality of your lives by supporting your health with nutritious food.

Color is used as a theme throughout this book to illustrate the bounty provided by nature and as a guide to healthy eating. Food color is indicative of health-enhancing phytonutrients that act as antioxidants to fight harmful chronic inflammation.

Phytonutrients occur naturally, but only in plants. These phytonutrients reduce our risk of those diseases associated with chronic inflammation, including cancer, atherosclerosis and diabetes.

Enjoying a variety of nutrient-rich whole plant foods that are good sources of naturally occurring fiber will ensure that you are maximizing your nutrient intake with delicious and tasty foods. Eating a full spectrum of colorful foods will provide you with health benefits and add variety, new tastes and excitement to your meals.

My food preparation ideas and variations are a combination of Gujarati cuisine and my desire for color, nutrition, taste, variety and convenience. (Gujarati culinary taste and style is lighter, more health-conscious and different from the traditional Indian cuisine featured in most Indian restaurants.) I use a variety of legumes and beans, grains, nuts and seeds and vegetables seasoned with herbs and spices. The recipes are mostly vegan and gluten-free (p.146); a few use yogurt.

This book comes with thanks to my adopted country of the United States (I relocated as a graduate student in nutrition in 1972), where I have learned much that has influenced my career and my cooking. With inspiration from my patients, students and colleagues I now share the confluence of traditional Indian heritage and Aryuvedic knowledge with modern health and food science.

As the French say *Bon appétit!,* so we Gujarati's say *Prem thee jamjo!* – which means, "Please eat with love and passion!"

Gita Patel MS RD CDE LD
Etna, New Hampshire
June 2011

Why "Feeding Health" is Important

Here is the science:

FREE RADICALS

Free radicals are a normal part of living. Eating and digesting food, for instance, generates free radicals. A free radical is an unstable oxygen molecule with an unpaired electron. Seeking stability, such molecules steal electrons from other molecules; disrupting their stability and causing chain reactions that produce even more free radicals. Free radicals cause damage to the DNA, cells and tissues, resulting in inflammation.[1,2] Inflammation is the underlying cause of ill health and most chronic diseases.

In addition to the free radicals produced by normal body processes, our cells are also exposed to free radicals from environmental sources – ultra-violet light, X-rays and other radiation, heat, cigarette smoke, alcohol and other pollutants. Excess exposure to free radicals without adequate antioxidant defenses can damage healthy cells, impact overall health and lead to early aging and cancer.[1,2] This is why we need to get plenty of antioxidants from our food everyday. Antioxidants inhibit the reactions of free radicals.

ANTIOXIDANTS

Antioxidants are compounds in whole, unprocessed, natural foods that can help scavenge free radicals by donating electrons to make them stable; reducing their activity and supporting health. Vitamins A (as beta-carotene), C and E and the mineral selenium, as well as certain plant nutrients (such as polyphenols) can act as antioxidants.

Antioxidants from nutrients in our diets are first-line defenders, suppressing oxygen free radicals and other reactive oxygen and nitrogen species that contribute to chronic diseases. They even repair damage caused by those radicals. Some antioxidants transform free radicals into less reactive compounds. Others stop the chemical processes that cancer-causing substances need to go through to become active. Scientists believe that an adequate supply of a variety of antioxidants, each carrying out a different protective role, may not only defend against cell changes that lead to disease, but also induce longevity, cell maintenance and DNA repair.[1,2]

Eating a variety of whole unprocessed plant foods through a diet rich in fruits, nuts and vegetables is important for obtaining the full spectrum of colorful and health-promoting combinations of antioxidants. We cannot store antioxidants in our bodies the way we can store some vitamins and minerals, so it is important to get them through our food every day.[1,2] Eating processed foods stripped of nutrients deprives you of a complete antioxidant team.

The following explanation was contributed by Dr. Thomas M. Wnorowski, Director of Medical Research; BodyBio, Inc.

If a person ingests an antioxidant food, such as the fat-soluble vitamin E (found in nuts) or the water-soluble vitamin C (found in citrus fruits), he or she can expect that antioxidant to donate one of its electrons to stabilize a free radical that can cause an illness or interrupt the normal function of the body. The causes of free radicals are hard to escape because they are all around us. Air pollution, vehicle exhausts, second-hand smoke and other outside-the-body insults are everywhere. Poor diet, illness and even a foul mood can create free radicals within the body.

Once an antioxidant gives up an electron, it becomes a free radical itself until another molecule gives up its own electron. This cycle continues on and on until the body's super-antioxidant, glutathione, comes to the rescue and donates an electron. Being a stable molecule, glutathione is not prone to becoming a free radical itself because its re-cycling capacity is encouraged by alpha-lipoic acid, a natural compound made by the body – especially from plant food – in sufficient amounts to help glutathione resist alterations. Alpha-lipoic acid is found in the chloroplasts of green foods such as broccoli, spinach and other leafy greens – the darker the greens the better!

Dr. Thomas M. Wnorowski

PHYTONUTRIENTS/PHYTOCHEMICALS:

Phyto comes from the Greek meaning "plant," and phytonutrients (also referred to as phytochemicals) are organic bioactive components of plants that promote health. Plant foods are rich in phytonutrients. Most phytonutrients have antioxidant properties that help our bodies fight harmful chronic inflammation, thus reducing our risk of diseases associated with chronic inflammation, including cancer, atherosclerosis, macular degeneration and diabetes. Phytonutrients disrupt established pro-inflammatory pathways.[3] Here are some examples of cancer fighting phytonutrients:

Indoles, phytonutrients found in cruciferous vegetables such as broccoli, cauliflower, cabbage and kale, stimulate enzymes that make the hormone estrogen less effective, possibly reducing the risk of hormone dependent breast cancer.

Isothiocyanates, found in these same vegetables, protect against cancer.

Allyl sulfides, in garlic and onions, also fight cancer.

Saponins in beans and other legumes may prevent cancer cells from multiplying by influencing genetic material in the cells.

Ellagic acid, a phenolic acid in strawberries and raspberries, reduces the genetic damage caused by carcinogens such as tobacco smoke or air pollution.

Lycopene, a carotenoid common in red vegetables such as tomatoes, pink grapefruit and papayas may help prevent several types of cancer and has beneficial effects on heart health.[1,2,3]

Contemporary Lifestyles and Chronic Diseases

Genes load the gun but lifestyle pulls the trigger.
– Elliott Joslin, M.D., founder of today's Joslin Diabetes Centers.

Today, some 125 million Americans live with chronic health conditions – including diabetes, obesity, heart disease, arthritis and cancer. Population Health Metrics, a journal of the Centers for Disease Control and Prevention, warns that one in three U.S. adults could have diabetes by 2050 if current trends continue. One in ten U.S adults have diabetes today; 25% do not know they have it. Fortunately, a healthy diet and physical activity can both reduce the risk of diabetes and help manage the condition.

As a society, we are losing the arts of cooking and enjoying meals with family and friends, eating slowly and relishing the food. We seem to be chronically short on time yet we have the same 24 hours in a day that our great-grandparents did. Eating is one of life's necessities and one of its great pleasures. Knowing how to cook and what to cook enhances our pleasure and gives us better health. This book will show you how to do this.

Health is something we do for ourselves, not something that is done to us; a journey rather than a destination; a dynamic, holistic, and purposeful way of living.

– Elliott Dacher, M.D.

Nature provides us with a variety of colorful foods that stimulate and satisfy all of our taste buds: sweet, salty, sour, pungent, bitter and astringent. But "advanced" food technology floods our grocery stores with processed convenience foods stripped of nutrients and fiber which has been replaced with fat, sugar and salt. We are influenced to choose foods devoid of color that do not stimulate all of our taste buds.

The science of Ayurveda traces most disease to an unbalanced diet. Good nutrition may not always be sufficient to treat and manage diseases that have already taken hold, but few diseases can be prevented without good nutrition. Whole plant foods play a major role in the prevention of chronic disease. Diabetes, cancer, heart disease, high blood pressure, arthritis, Alzheimer's disease and osteoporosis develop silently and painlessly. Usually, we don't know we have the diseases until they are well advanced and symptoms have developed.

I am making the case for mindful home cooking as the best way to feed health. The substances in whole foods exist in a complex balance that cannot be reproduced in a pill or in heavily processed foods. Cooking with fresh ingredients is both nutritious and economical. It is also helpful for those with celiac disease (p.146), food allergies, food intolerances or delayed food sensitivities requiring special diets.

Cooking is a matter of trusting yourself. It can be an exciting adventure in observing, tasting, touching, smelling and hearing the ingredients as you cook them, combining taste and health deliciously on the plate. Gujarati cuisine lets you spice up your meals while keeping them simple and flavorful. If you do not enjoy hot peppers you can reduce or eliminate them.

Preparing Indian food is not an exact science. When I teach Indian cooking, I stress the importance of not fixating on following the exact recipe all the time. Once you have a variety of ingredients on hand and have learned the basics of how to use the spices, you can be flexible and creative. You can cook every recipe in this book successfully even if you are missing an ingredient or two. Substitutions are listed; allow yourself to be creative.

Let your cooking reflect our multicultural society and our contemporary lifestyles.

I have provided nutrient analysis for the recipes for your education and awareness. However, this book is not another fad diet book about counting calories, carbohydrates, fats or proteins. It is about a healthful lifestyle, about enjoying eating whole plant foods high in nutrient density, low in calorie density and high in volume, so that you feel satisfied and not hungry. It is about colorful foods high in fiber and phytonutrients. As you transition to a healthful plant-based diet, you will notice the colors on your plate, enjoy the aromas and taste the flavors from the variety of herbs and spices used in the dishes you are now consuming.

Eating habits are formed early in life. Changing old habits takes time and effort. Nonetheless, I believe that if you eat in this healthful way, you will consume more nutrients, lose weight, feel more energetic and lower your risk for chronic disease. The food choice and preparation ideas that follow will help you eat more nutrient-rich plant foods that are delicious and simple to produce while you learn to use herbs and spices creatively. Most importantly you will learn that cooking can be fun.

Readers should be aware that knowledge of nutrition and medicine is constantly evolving. However, the basics of eating a variety of colorful whole foods are time-tested. If you are healthy, this book will help you stay healthy and reduce your risk for succumbing to the chronic diseases of our time. If you have a chronic disease, this book will give you the tools to manage your disease better.

If you are ready to maintain or improve the quality of your life, turn the page. Our first stop is the kitchen, where you will learn to organize your cooking space; our next stop will be the pantry, where you will learn to stock efficiently. You will soon be able to turn your kitchen into an "instant take-out place" for healthy food.

To administer medicine to diseases which have already developed and thereby suppress bodily chaos which has already occurred is comparable to the behavior of those who would begin to dig a well after they had grown thirsty, or those who would begin to cast weapons after they have engaged in a battle. Would these actions not be too late?

– Huang Di 400 B.C.

Planning for Success – Organizing the Kitchen

Surviving is important. Thriving is elegant.

– Maya Angelou

Cooking is a healing and nourishing act. It benefits you and those you love and cook for. Expensive or elaborate equipment isn't necessary, but awareness is crucial. View your cooking as a form of meditation in which you are using wholesome, nourishing ingredients with an understanding of their healing properties.

It is not necessary to sacrifice convenience to prepare and eat healthful vegetarian meals.

With planning you can make time for food preparation. For example, one of my patients decided to collaborate with a group of five friends. Every week they took turns preparing the main dish while the other 4 friends provided the accompanying salads or vegetable side dishes.

Delegate to family members. A pediatrician in my cooking class worked long days in addition to teaching at the medical school. I was surprised when she announced that she was able to cook Indian vegetarian food several times a week. During the weekend she planned, delegating the food preparation steps to her children and husband. Each one made a small contribution towards the final product and when she returned home after a long workday, everything was sliced, diced, minced and prepared so that cooking an Indian meal was a snap. Often, on the weekend, she would get together with friends to cook for the week, share a meal together and take home food for the rest of the week.

Make your kitchen an instant take-out place for healthy food! If the pantry, kitchen, refrigerator and freezer are well stocked and organized for convenience and nutrition, feeding health is easy and fast.

I have provided simple nutritious food preparation instructions at the start of each food category. You can build your pantry inventory over a period of time using the list below. Personal preferences and your family's likes and dislikes will influence what and how much you stock from the list I have provided. Once you have what you need on hand, you can enjoy being creative in the kitchen.

For efficient food preparation, organize your kitchen along these lines:

1. Pressure cookers, rice cookers and slow cookers (crock pots) save time and attention when cooking rice and beans.
2. A food processor saves time grating and chopping.
3. A blender or hand-blender makes puréeing easier.

4. An area of the kitchen counter kept routinely clear for food preparation saves wear and tear on your nerves and prevents a lot of spills.

5. Appliances used frequently – food processor, blender, electric hand blender, for instance – should be kept easily accessible.

6. Frequently-used ingredients and utensils should be stored as close to hand as possible; those used less frequently can go on high shelves or in the backs of deep cupboards.

7. Herbs and spices should be stored conveniently, but not too close to the stove as they lose flavor when too warm. A drawer beside the stove is ideal.

8. A master list of your basic pantry staples kept in a convenient place will help you know when certain foods are running out and need replacing.

TIMESAVING TIPS

1. After grocery shopping wash, cut and wrap up vegetables to give you a head start. Mushrooms, cucumbers and fresh ginger should be stored in the refrigerator in paper, waxed paper or cloth bags, not plastic. This allows them to breathe and prevents them from spoiling too quickly. Wash leafy greens, carrots, turnips and radishes; wrap them while still damp in a dishtowel, then put the wrapped bundle in a plastic bag and refrigerate.

2. Double the vegetables you prepare for dinner and use the extras for lunch the next day, reheated or as part of a different recipe.

3. Roast a big batch of different vegetables such as cubed white or sweet potatoes, beets, carrots, winter squash, onions, turnips and parsnips and use them for several side dishes or lunches during the week – cold as a salad, reheated or prepared in another recipe. To roast vegetables, mix the cut vegetables with a little olive oil and your favorite dried or fresh herbs and spices, add a couple of peeled garlic cloves (delicious when roasted!), and bake in a single layer on rimmed baking sheets at 400°F for 30 - 45 minutes or longer, stirring once or twice during the cooking, until vegetables are tender or as desired.

4. Keep frozen vegetables in the freezer for convenience. Research shows they are nearly as nutritious as fresh vegetables.

5. For Indian spice mixtures, use your food processor efficiently: mince any nuts first, remove the nuts, then process the ginger and remove, then process the hot green chili peppers and remove and finally process the garlic. Now you only have to wash the food processor once! Spice mixtures will last five days in the refrigerator, but they also freeze well.

   Freeze them in zip lock bags, flattening the bag to under 1/8" thick so you can break off just the amount you need and return the rest to the freezer.

   You can also freeze spice mixtures in small ice cube trays. Place the frozen cubes in a plastic freezer bag and take out exactly what you need at a later time.

   Always date and label foods you freeze.

6. Multitasking saves time! While preparing dinner, place a pot of soaked beans to cook on the back burner. They require little preparation time and can be used for

another meal. When you soak dried beans for a recipe, soak and cook extra for the freezer. Soaking instructions are provided on page 70, first tip.

7. Choose one day or evening each week to cook ingredients for several meals.

8. Use all burners on your stove top at once, plus the oven, for cooking extras to refrigerate and freeze.

9. When you cook beans and grains, cook more than one variety in separate pots. You can keep some to build on the rest of the week while freezing the rest for later use. To freeze cooked beans or grains, spread them on a baking sheet lined with waxed paper or plastic wrap. Freeze 15 minutes, then transfer the beans or grains to freezer jars or bags, label and date them, and store them in the freezer. This will keep the beans from sticking together so you can easily pour out just the amount you need later.

10. Prepare recipes in stages. Peel garlic or wash, trim and cut vegetables for the next day with the family after dinner while you all talk. You can create some wonderful family memories this way. Store the prepared vegetables in the refrigerator to use within the next day or two. Store peeled fresh garlic in a glass jar in the refrigerator. Use it within 7-10 days.

11. Cover pots to bring water to a boil more quickly.

12. Before beginning a recipe prepare all ingredients and arrange them on a counter near the stove.

Basic Staples – Stocking the Kitchen

IN THE PANTRY

Beans, Legumes, Peas

Stock a colorful variety of dried beans (keep on hand a few cans of your family's favorite varieties for convenience).

Small dark red adzuki beans, black beans, black-eyed peas, white cannellini beans, golden chickpeas (garbanzo beans), maroon cranberry beans, brown fava beans, green flageolets, white great northern beans, dark red kidney beans, light pink kidney beans, green, brown or black lentils, ivory lima beans, green mung beans, white navy beans, small white beans, white pea beans, speckled red pinto beans, red beans, pale yellow-green soybeans, split green peas and split yellow peas.

Grains

Stock colorful whole grains and grain flours. Light gold amaranth, pale brown barley, rich brown buckwheat flour and buckwheat groats, beige Japanese soba noodles, golden or white corn grits, ivory rolled oats, golden millet, red and golden quinoa, light brown or white basmati rice, gluten-free hot and cold cereals your family needs and likes, pasta and crackers your family likes.

Nuts and Seeds

Nuts and seeds and their butters provide a wide range of colors: light brown almonds and almond butter, cream-colored raw cashews and light brown cashew butter, dark brown Brazil nuts, golden-brown chestnuts, tan or red-skinned peanuts and brown peanut butter, golden-brown filberts (hazelnuts), cream-colored macadamia nuts, brown pecans, ivory pine nuts, green pistachios, golden walnuts, gray poppy seeds, light gold and black sesame seeds and tan tahini, sage green pumpkin seeds, light brown sunflower seeds and sunflower butter and white coconut – shredded, dried and unsweetened.

Vegetables

All of these vegetables can be kept without refrigeration for days or weeks in a cool pantry bin or even on the counter. Note, however, that potatoes exposed to light quickly develop a green color, which indicates the presence of solanine, a mild human poison. You can store potatoes in the pantry in a small closed cardboard box or shoebox to keep them in the dark. Red and yellow onions, white or pink-streaked garlic, orange yams, yellow, russet, green and blue winter squashes, brown-skinned white and yellow baking potatoes, red-skinned white and yellow boiling potatoes, white and orange sweet potatoes, deep red, orange and pink beets, purple-topped white turnips, purple-topped golden rutabagas, bright-red canned tomatoes and paste and bright-red canned vegetable or tomato juice.

Herbs and Spices

Stock a variety of colors of ground spices in small quantities in little glass jars with tight-fitting lids – or keep whole spices and dried herbs on hand and grind them fresh in a coffee grinder or spice grinder, as you need them.

Black mustard seeds and coarsely ground gold mustard; brown cumin seeds and powder; light brown coriander seeds and powder; tan fenugreek seeds; brown cinnamon sticks and powder; cardamom pods and powder; dark gray ajwain seeds; yellow turmeric powder; brown curry powder or garam masala; white asafetida powder; allspice, whole and powder; red cayenne or chili pepper, whole and ground; green bay leaves; green dill leaves, dried; beige ginger powder; brown fennel seeds, whole and powder; burnt orange mace, ground; green parsley, dried; green oregano, dried; green mint, dried; green sage, ground; green thyme, whole leaf and powder and green tarragon.

Condiments

Vinegars for salad dressing; canned sauces, unopened; vegetable juices, unopened; sea salt and healthy snack foods

IN THE REFRIGERATOR

Store washed and cut vegetables in sealed containers in the refrigerator so they are ready when you need them. Fruit, with the exception of berries, can also be washed and refrigerated. Fresh greens; fresh vegetables; peeled garlic; fresh herbs – dill, cilantro, parsley, basil, thyme, mint, tarragon etc.; lemons, limes and fresh fruits; opened jars of nut butters; flax seeds, golden and brown; healthy beverages; yogurt, dairy or non-dairy; milk, dairy or non-dairy; tofu and tempeh; condiments – vinegars, sauces and cooked leftovers. Whenever you can, buy cold-pressed vegetable oils of the varieties your family likes best. If not used daily store them in the refrigerator to prevent rancidity. Oils – olive, flaxseed, sesame, walnut, peanut, corn, canola, safflower or grape seed oil.

IN THE FREEZER

Make it your instant take-out place! Label and date all foods in the freezer. Then you can enjoy a healthy vegetarian meal within minutes when time becomes an issue. You can be spontaneous and enjoy cooking if ingredients are handy and ready to be used. Vegetables, fruits, nuts and seeds (store large quantities in the freezer to prevent rancidity and pour out smaller amounts in smaller containers kept in the pantry for easy accessibility), tahini (sesame seed butter), hummus, pesto, fresh ginger (easy to grate when frozen), fresh herbs minced, cooked grains, beans and legumes and leftover and pre planned cooked foods

Bean Flours

Bean flours need refrigerating or freezing to prevent the oils in them from going rancid. Chickpea flour, mung bean flour and soybean flour are available and a good idea to keep on hand.

Important Questions

Should I worry about salt?

The *2010 Dietary Guidelines for Americans* recommends that adults reduce their daily sodium (salt) intake to 1,500 mg to manage and prevent high blood pressure.[4] This translates into approximately 1 tsp of salt each day, depending on the brand used. The sodium content per gram of different brands varies considerably. For example, 1 teaspoon of diamond crystal kosher salt weighs 2.8 gm, and contains 1120 mg sodium. A teaspoon of Morton Salt Balance (contains 25% less sodium due to the addition of potassium chloride) weighs 6 g, and contains 1760 mg sodium.

My recipes can all be prepared without salt for people with salt sensitivity or high blood pressure. You can also try sodium-free salt substitutes such as "No Salt" or Mrs. Dash's sodium-free salt. It is important to note that whole unprocessed plant foods in their natural state do not contain much sodium, so adding a little iodized salt during the cooking process contributes to taste as well as providing the essential nutrient iodine. Athletic people who sweat a lot and are not salt sensitive may need to add salt to their food.

In addition to limiting salt in the diet, high blood pressure can also be managed by increasing potassium intake. Eat plenty of fruits, vegetables, legumes and whole grains to increase potassium in your diet. Most excess sodium comes from restaurant foods and processed foods, including breakfast cereals and common condiments such as mustard and ketchup. To avoid added salt as well as added fats, cook more meals from scratch at home, seek out potassium-rich foods and flavor foods with herbs and spices.

Together, herbs and spices are a powerhouse of antioxidants. I tend to use herbs liberally, both for flavor and the antioxidant nutrients they provide. If you prefer, you may substitute any other herb for the cilantro that I use in the recipes that follow. Using herbs and spices creatively helps cut back on added fat and salt.

Using lemon or lime for flavoring provides several benefits. I use lemon and lime juice freely for taste, nutrition and to replace some or all of the salt in a recipe. Citrus fruits provide vitamin C, increase the absorption of calcium and iron, are alkaline in the body and add some sour taste to food, which makes salt less necessary. Lemons in particular contain monoterpenoids, such as d-limonene, which assist the body in detoxifying itself.[5,6] Experiment by adding a little lemon, lime or orange zest to your food. Add some zest to plain water for a fresh flavor plus added nutrition.

What About Protein?

Protein requirements are based on ideal body weight: daily, 0.8 g protein per kilogram of body weight for ages 19 years and older. According to the 2010 dietary guidelines for Americans, "plant-based diets are able to meet protein requirements for essential amino acids and offer other potential benefits, such as sources of fiber and nutrients important in a health-promoting diet."[4]

Proteins, carbohydrates and fats are macronutrients. Current recommendations for macronutrient distributions are:

Protein: 15%-20% of total calories

Carbohydrates: 50%-55% of the total calories

Fats: 30% or less of total calories, 7% or less may be saturated fat

Fiber: The American Dietetic Association recommends a minimum of 20–35 grams per day for a healthy adult depending on calorie intake; about 14 gm per 1000 calories.[7]

Consider these reassuring statistics:

Grains on average provide 12% protein calories.

Beans and legumes on average provide 22% to 25% protein calories.

Soy provides even higher percent protein calories.

Non-starchy vegetables on average are 40% or higher in protein calories.

Nuts and seeds on average provide 12% -15% protein calories, are very low in carbohydrates and high in beneficial fats.

Do you recommend a fat-free diet?

No. Fat serves many important functions in the body, one of them being the absorption of fat-soluble vitamins. Your body needs fat; however, not all fats are equally beneficial. Trans-fats should always be avoided. Plant foods such as nuts, seeds and avocado are good sources of both monounsaturated and polyunsaturated healthful fats, which do not contain any cholesterol or trans-fats.

What if I am allergic to some foods?

Individuals with delayed food sensitivities, food intolerances and allergies or dislikes for certain foods can easily make selections from the lists of substitutions included with most of the recipes that follow. Anyone with food allergies or delayed food sensitivities must consult their healthcare provider and registered dietitian for personalized medical assistance.

Introduction to Cooking & Recipes

Vaghar (hot oil seasoning)

Most of my recipes start the same way; with a simple seasoning of spices, oil, food to be cooked with a little water, called in Gujarati a vaghar. Cooking activates the aromatic oils in seeds and spices, which the oil and water capture. Vaghar enhances the flavors of food when you cut back on salt and fat. Adding a whole dried hot red chili pepper to the spices in a vaghar will flavor the food even more. Discard the peppers before serving if you like.

The traditional Gujarati method puts seeds and spices in hot oil alone. I have modified this practice for health reasons. When oil reaches its smoking point its nutritional quality is reduced, because of increased production of acrylamides, so I add one to two tablespoons of water to the food to be cooked with the oil. To prevent splattering add the food ingredient with the water to the oil. Traditional Gujarati cooking uses any of the following oils – corn, canola, peanut, sesame, safflower, sunflower or other vegetable oils. The recipes in this book were analyzed for canola oil and olive oil but you may use any cooking oil of your choice. Here is an example of a simple vaghar for potatoes:

INGREDIENTS:

Cumin Seeds	½ t
Olive oil	2 T
Asafetida (a resin, known as hing)	a pinch
Potatoes diced	2 Cups
Water	2 T
Turmeric	¼ t
Salt	to taste or ¼ t

DIRECTIONS:

1. Assemble and prepare all ingredients.
2. In a heavy-bottomed 1-quart skillet or pan heat cumin seeds on medium high.
3. Just as the seeds begin to give off a roasted aroma and before they pop or burn, add oil, a pinch of hing and diced potatoes with water.
4. Stir and turn heat down to medium; and add turmeric and salt.
5. Stir and cook covered until potatoes are tender. Add more water if necessary to prevent scorching.

After the initial vaghar the recipes vary. Once you have mastered vaghar, it is easy to make any Gujarati food. The seeds and spices combinations for vaghar are many; you can choose the flavor combinations you prefer from the list of vaghar on page 137.

You can add some ground flax seeds at the end of the cooking process to most of the recipes that follow.

Vegetables:

Of all foods, vegetables offer the most diversity in color, taste, texture, shape and size. Vegetables are important because they are nutrient-dense and good sources of fiber, yet naturally very low in calories. Nutrient-dense means they provide more nutrients than calories per gram of the vegetable. Vegetables supply nearly all of the vitamins, minerals, fiber, antioxidants, phytonutrients and protein required for feeding health. Non-starchy vegetables provide an average of 40% or more calories from protein. Starchy vegetables such as potatoes and winter squash provide complex carbohydrates for energy.[8] Vegetables contain no cholesterol, have very little fat and are low in calories. Enjoying these colorful and tasty foods is a great way to feed health and lose weight. This is why my serving sizes for vegetables are larger, ranging between ¾ cup to over 1 cup.

Vegetables are alkaline, and alkali-producing plant foods may help preserve bone and muscle mass as well as help reduce the acid load, which accompanies the typical high-protein diet from animal foods. This may be a key to maintaining bone health and muscle mass in older adults.[6]

Vegetables provide sweet tastes (winter squash, beets), bitter tastes (dark leafy greens), astringent tastes (asparagus), pungent tastes (watercress) and salty tastes (celery). They combine well with most other foods, including beans, grains, yogurt, nuts and seeds. They afford us a wide variety of combinations to feed health.

Vegetable Classification

Vegetables are classified by the part of the plant that is eaten. I included this section to highlight the colors, flavors and nutrients supplied by each group. This should also help you increase your cooking and eating enjoyment by including more variety in your meals. You could have a weekly goal to include vegetables from each group.

Dark Green Leafy Vegetables (DGLV)

Spinach, swiss chard, salad greens, collard greens, kale, bok choy, radicchio, and watercress contain lots of water and few carbohydrates or calories. They are excellent sources of beta-carotene and vitamin C, good sources of fiber and folic acid, with varying amounts of iron and calcium, as well as being high in antioxidant nutrients and phytonutrients. A few leafy greens are actually the tops of root vegetables, such as turnips, radishes, and beets. The kales, collards, arugula, dandelion, chicory, endives, turnip and mustard greens (especially this last) also contribute pungent and bitter tastes.[8]

Flowers, Buds and Stalks

Celery, broccoli, cauliflower, asparagus and artichokes are rich in vitamin C, calcium, potassium and phytonutrients as well as fiber. Cauliflower and broccoli may protect against cancer.[8]

Seeds and Pods

Snap beans, green beans, lima beans, peas and sweet corn contain more protein and carbohydrate than the leafy vegetables. They are good sources of B vitamins, zinc, potassium, magnesium, calcium and iron in addition to their phytonutrients.[8]

Roots, Bulbs and Tubers

Onions, turnips, white and sweet potatoes, yams, beets, carrots, radishes and parsnips grow partly or wholly underground and are nutrient storehouses with higher starch content than other vegetables. They are good sources of vitamin C and potassium. Sweet potatoes and carrots provide beta-carotene; radishes and turnips provide vitamin C and fiber. Research suggests that onions and garlic may lower blood pressure and cholesterol.[8]

Fruit Vegetables

Eggplant, squashes, peppers, okras and tomatoes tend to be good sources of vitamin C, phytonutrients and fiber. They offer a wonderful variety of colors, textures and flavors.[8]

Cruciferous or Brassica Vegetables

Cabbage, broccoli, brussels sprouts, cauliflower, kale, collards, arugula, mustard and turnip greens, rutabagas, turnips and radishes fall into more than one classification and are also in this group. Brassicas contain nitrogen compounds called indoles, which protect against certain forms of cancer. Kale, collards and turnip greens supply calcium, while brussels sprouts provide protein, potassium and iron.[8]

Vegetables

Edamame with Stir-fried Vegetables

Simple – Serves 6

Edamame (Green Soybean or Sweet Soybean) has been cultivated in China for over 3,000 years. Research shows that consuming isoflavone-containing whole soy foods, as opposed to isolated isoflavones, significantly inhibits bone loss and stimulates bone formation in menopausal women. Whole soy foods protect post-menopausal women against cardiovascular disease. Soybeans, high in protein, contain molybdenum, iron, manganese, phosphorus, omega-3 fatty acids, magnesium, copper, potassium, vitamin B2 and choline.[8,9,10]
For a video of cooking this recipe go to www.feedinghealth.com.

INGREDIENTS:

Olive oil	2 T
Cumin seeds	1 t
Garlic chopped	3 cloves
Jalapeño pepper sliced in half	one-half
Corn kernels fresh (or frozen)	1½ Cups
Turmeric	¼ t
Salt	to taste or ¼ t
Edamame thawed	1 Cup
Zucchini diced	3 Cups
Sweet red bell pepper diced	1 Cup
Cilantro with tender stems chopped	1 Cup
Lemon juiced	one-half

DIRECTIONS:

1. Assemble and prepare all ingredients.
2. Add jalapeño, salt and turmeric to the corn and set it aside.
3. Heat on medium-high heat a 2 to 3 quart skillet or pan. Add cumin seeds.
4. When the seeds begin to change color add oil and garlic, turn heat to medium.
5. Fry the garlic for a minute, then add corn with combined ingredients. Stir and cook covered for 2 to 3 minutes.
6. Stir and add edamame, zucchini and red pepper. Stir and cook covered for 3 to 4 minutes.
7. Before serving add chopped cilantro and fresh lemon juice, stirring to mix all the ingredients.
8. Serve the vegetables over rice, quinoa or millet as part of a meal. Enjoy leftovers for lunch in a pita pocket.

NUTRITION INFORMATION PER SERVING:
Calories: 128 **Protein:** 5 g **Total Carbohydrates:** 16 g
Fiber: 3 g **Total Fat:** 6 g **Sodium:** 59 mg
Calcium: 46 mg **Omega-3 Fats (ALA):** 80 mg

VARIATIONS & OPTIONS

- Eliminate jalapeño if you prefer it without the heat of the pepper. Substitute cayenne pepper, fresh ground black pepper or mild paprika for the jalapeño.

- Substitute chopped onion for garlic.

- Substitute either basil or parsley for cilantro.

- The recipe calls for 6 ½ cups of vegetables, so you can substitute a variety of vegetable combinations.

- Substitute 1-cup sprouts for 1-cup zucchini.

- Substitute canned beans for edamame.

Cabbage Stir-fried Salad

Simple – Serves 8

Cabbage contains sulforaphane, isothiocyanate and indoles, phytochemicals that enhance the breakdown and excretion of cancer-causing compounds in the liver; vitamins C, K, A, B, folate; as well as the minerals manganese, potassium, calcium and magnesium.[8,9,10]

INGREDIENTS:

Cumin seeds	1 t
Canola oil	3 T
Sugar snap peas	(½ lb trimmed) 2 Cup
Sesame seeds	2 T
Red bell peppers cut in 1-½" pieces	(½ lb trimmed) 2 Cups
Savoy cabbage shredded 1 lb	8 Cups
Salt	to taste or ½ t
Red chili pepper	to taste or ½ t
Turmeric	½ t
Lemon zest	¼ t
Lemon juiced	one-half
Cilantro chopped with tender stems	1 Cup

DIRECTIONS:

1. Assemble and prepare all ingredients.
2. Combine shredded cabbage, salt, red chili pepper, turmeric and lemon zest.
3. Add sesame seeds to the sugar snap peas.
4. Heat cumin seeds in a 5-quart pan or skillet on high heat. When the seeds give off an aroma and are toasted add oil and sugar snap peas with sesame seeds.
5. Stir and cook on medium high heat for 2 to 3 minutes.
6. Add red peppers, stir and cook 2-3 minutes.
7. Add cabbage with combined ingredients, stir and cook for 2 -3 minutes.
8. Turn heat off and add cilantro and lemon juice. Stir to mix all ingredients.
9. Serve with rice, beans, millet or quinoa.

VARIATIONS & OPTIONS

- Substitute a yukon gold potato diced in small cubes for 4 cups of shredded cabbage. In step 4 after the seeds have toasted add diced potato with 2 T water and oil. Stir and cook covered for 3 to 4 minutes on medium high heat, stirring occasionally, till the potato is almost tender. Then follow the recipe with rest of the ingredients and steps.

- Substitute black mustard seeds for cumin seeds.

- Substitute bok choy or green, red or napa cabbage for savoy cabbage.

- Substitute snow peas, sprouts, edamame or cooked chickpeas for part of the cabbage.

- Substitute parsley or dill for cilantro.

- Substitute coconut or any other nut or seeds (flax seeds) for sesame seeds.

- Substitute any other hot pepper for the red chili pepper.

- Add 2 - 3 sliced garlic cloves in step 4 with oil, sugar snap peas and sesame seeds.

NUTRITION INFORMATION PER SERVING:
Calories: 119 **Protein:** 4 g **Total Carbohydrates:** 14 g
Fiber: 6 g **Total Fat:** 6.5 g **Sodium:** 113 mg
Calcium: 98 mg **Omega-3 Fats (ALA):** 550 mg

Carrots Stir-fried with Sprouts and Vegetables

Simple – Serves 6

Carrots contain vitamins A, C and K and the mineral potassium. Carrots and colored peppers contain beta-carotene, which is best absorbed when consumed with some fat.[8,9,10]

INGREDIENTS:

Carrots – grated, **Green cabbage** – shredded, **Scallions** – sliced, **Colored peppers** – diced	4 Cups
Mung beans sprouts packed	2 Cups
Canola oil	2 T
Black mustard seeds	½ t
Asafetida (hing)	pinch
Coconut dry, shredded, unsweetened	2 T
Salt	to taste or ⅛ t
Turmeric	⅓ t
Cayenne pepper	¼ t
Cilantro chopped with tender stems	½ Cup
Lemon juice	1 T

DIRECTIONS:

1. Assemble and prepare all ingredients.
2. Combine vegetables, sprouts, coconut, salt, turmeric and cayenne; set aside.
3. Heat mustard seeds in a 2-quart pan or skillet.
4. Before the seeds begin to pop, add oil, asafetida and vegetables with combined ingredients, stir well and cook for 5 minutes or to taste.
5. Add cilantro and lemon juice before serving.
6. Serve as a salad with a meal. It goes well with rice or khichadi (p. 94)
7. Use leftovers as a filling in a pita pocket or a wrap.

VARIATIONS & OPTIONS

- Add a large yukon gold potato to this recipe. Wash and dice the potato. After adding asafetida to the vaghar in step 4, add the potato with 2 T of water; cook covered for about 5 minutes before adding the rest of the ingredients and follow the steps in the recipe.

- Use a combination of cabbage with grated carrots, or a combination of
    - Cabbage, grated carrots and frozen green peas
    - Cabbage, grated carrots and diced potato
    - Cabbage, grated carrots, diced potato and peas, corn or edamame

- Combine 4 cups carrots with the 2 cups mung bean, soy or lentil sprouts.

- Combine carrots and cooked chickpeas (so you get the crunch of carrots with the softness of the chickpeas) – or any other cooked bean or lentil.

- Substitute soy or lentil sprouts for mung bean sprouts.

NUTRITION INFORMATION PER SERVING:

Calories: 89 **Protein:** 2 g **Total Carbohydrates:** 8 g
Fiber: 3 g **Total Fat:** 6 g **Sodium:** 48 mg
Calcium: 32 mg **Omega-3 Fats (ALA):** 460 mg

www.FeedingHealth.com

Cauliflower

Simple – Serves 4

Cauliflower contains vitamins B1, B2, B3, B5, B6, C, K and folate; minerals such as manganese, potassium, phosphorus and magnesium, as well as sulforaphane, isothiocyanate and indoles (phytochemicals that enhance the breakdown and excretion of cancer-causing compounds in the liver). Cauliflower provides nutrient support for the body's detoxification system, its antioxidant system and its inflammatory/anti-inflammatory system, all closely connected with cancer development.[5,8,9,10]

INGREDIENTS:

Cinnamon . . . . 1 stick
Cloves whole 4
Green cardamoms, whole 3
Canola oil . . . . 1 T
Tomato, large diced 1
Cauliflower bite size pieces . . . . 4 Cups
Cumin ground . . . . 1 t
Coriander ground . . . . 2 t
Cayenne pepper . . . . to taste or ⅛ t
Turmeric . . . . ½ t
Salt . . . . ¼ t
Cashew nuts ground . . . . 3 T
Cilantro chopped, for garnish . . . . ½ Cup

DIRECTIONS:

1. Assemble and prepare all ingredients.
2. Heat a heavy-bottomed 2-quart pan with cinnamon stick, cloves and whole cardamom pods broken open slightly.
3. When the cloves begin to give out their aroma and darken add the oil and tomato, stir, and cook for 1 to 2 minutes.
4. Add cauliflower stir and cook covered till crisp tender.
5. Add coriander and cumin powders, cayenne, turmeric, salt and cashews. Mix well and turn heat off.
6. Garnish with cilantro and serve with a meal containing a grain and/or beans or a khichadi (p. 94)

VARIATIONS & OPTIONS

- Add ¼ t black mustard seeds to the vaghar in addition to or in place of the cinnamon, cloves and cardamom.

- Substitute ground flax seeds, shredded coconut or ground walnuts or almonds for cashews.

- Add green peas and diced potatoes to the cauliflower, adjusting the amounts of the spices if the quantity of vegetables is greater than 4 cups. Add cut potato first in step 4; allow the potato to cook for 4 minutes before adding the cauliflower. Add peas when cauliflower is almost cooked.

- Add 1 to 2 cups of sprouts and cook with cauliflower.

- Add 1 to 2 cups chopped dill 5 minutes after you have added cauliflower.

- Try these combinations:
  - Cauliflower with peas, corn, zucchini or bean sprouts
  - Cauliflower, diced tomatoes, corn and shelled edamame
  - Cauliflower with dill and onions
  - Cauliflower with spinach, corn and diced tomatoes
  - Cauliflower with cooked chickpeas, cannellini beans, lentils or black beans
  - Cauliflower with chopped onion, diced tomato and peeled and diced sweet potato

- If you are using fresh vegetables and intend to freeze some, under cook the amount you plan to freeze.

NUTRITION INFORMATION PER SERVING:
Calories: 110 **Protein:** 4 g **Total Carbohydrates:** 10 g
Fiber: 4 g **Total Fat:** 7 g **Sodium:** 106 mg
Calcium: 47 mg **Omega-3 Fats (ALA):** 430 mg

Dill with Split Mung Beans

Simple – Serves 4

Dill leaves are rich in beta-carotene, iron and potassium. Dill seed is a good source of calcium, manganese and iron as well as important phytonutrients. (8,9,10)

INGREDIENTS:

Dill greens with tender stems, chopped, packed... 4 Cups (3 ounces)
Split mung beans soaked in water for 30 minutes . . . . ½ Cup
Water . . . . 1 Cup
Canola oil . . . . 1 T
Asafetida (hing) . . . . pinch
Garlic sliced. . . . . .3 cloves
Turmeric . . . . ½ t
Cayenne or chili pepper. . . . . to taste or ⅛ t
Salt . . . . to taste or ⅛ t
Lemon or lime juiced. . . . . one-half

DIRECTIONS:

1. Assemble and prepare all ingredients.

2. Heat a 2-quart pan on medium-high heat. Add sliced garlic, asafetida and oil. Fry the garlic for about a minute.

3. Add soaked, drained beans, 1-cup water and turmeric; bring to a boil, reduce heat and simmer covered for 7 minutes. (If mung beans have not been soaked, cook covered for 12 minutes.)

4. Add salt, cayenne and dill; stir and cook 5-7 minutes till beans are tender.

5. Add lemon or limejuice before serving.

6. Serve with a grain such as rice, millet or quinoa as part of a meal.

VARIATIONS & OPTIONS

- If you like this dish to have a sauce add 1 ¼ to 1½ cups water with the beans.

- Substitute any canned beans, lentils or tuver daal for the soaked split mung beans; tuver daal takes longer to cook so allow longer cooking time before adding dill.

- Substitute cut-up cauliflower or diced potatoes for the beans.

- Add sunflower seeds, sesame seeds or pumpkin seeds with sliced garlic and diced potatoes, stir-frying a few minutes to cook the potato partially before adding dill.

NUTRITION INFORMATION PER SERVING:

Calories: 101 **Protein:** 5 g **Total Carbohydrates:** 13 g
Fiber: 3 g **Total Fat:** 4 g **Sodium:** 45 mg
Calcium: 50 mg **Omega-3 Fats (ALA):** 330 mg

Beets

INGREDIENTS:

Beets washed, unpeeled 5

DIRECTIONS:

1. Trim the ends of the whole unpeeled beets.
2. Boil or roast them whole.
3. When beets are cool enough to handle, peel and slice them. Enjoy with a meal or in a salad.

Beets Sweet and Sour

Beets contain lycopene which research shows reduces the risk of several types of cancer, including prostate cancer. Beets contain betalains; phytonutrients, which provide antioxidant, anti-inflammatory and detoxification support to the body.[8,9,10]

INGREDIENTS:

Beets peeled, cubed. . . . . .4 Cups
Black mustard seeds . . . . ½ t
Asafetida (hing) . . . . pinch
Canola oil . . . . .4 t
Jalapeño pepper sliced in half . . . . ½
Onion red, medium, chopped 1
Water . . . . .2-3 T
Turmeric. . . . . ½ t
Salt. . . . . to taste or ¼ t
Coconut shredded, dried, unsweetened. . . . . 1 T
Lemon juiced. . . . . ½
Cilantro with tender stems, chopped . . . . ½ Cup

DIRECTIONS:

1. Assemble and prepare all ingredients.
2. Heat the mustard seeds in a heavy-bottomed 3-quart pan.
3. When the seeds change color and before they pop, add oil, asafetida, jalapeño and onion; sauté for 1 minute.
4. Add cubed beets, water, turmeric and salt; stir and cook covered on medium heat till beets are tender. Stir twice during cooking.
5. Add coconut, lemon juice and cilantro.
6. Serve as part of a meal, warm or cold.
   Note: Leftovers freeze well.

NUTRITION INFORMATION PER SERVING:

Calories: 62 **Protein:** 1 gram **Total Carbohydrates:** 8 g
Fiber: 2 g **Total Fat:** 3 g **Sodium:** 90 mg
Calcium: 17 mg **Omega-3 Fats (ALA):** 220 mg

VARIATIONS & OPTIONS

- Substitute slivered almonds, cashews, ground flax seeds, sesame or sunflower seeds for the coconut.

- When the beets are half-cooked – or almost cooked if you like your sprouts crisp – add 1 to 2 cups of sprouted mung beans, lentils, Chinese bean or soy sprouts or 2 cups thawed frozen edamame beans.

- From step 4 on in this recipe, beets may be roasted in the oven. Omit water if roasting beets in the oven. When beets are tender add coconut, lemon juice and cilantro.

- Substitute any other root vegetable for beets in this recipe.

Spinach Stir-fry
Simple – Serves 4

Spinach contains beta-carotene; vitamins B2, B6, C, K, E and folic acid and varying amounts of the minerals magnesium, manganese, calcium, iron, potassium, phosphorus, copper, selenium and zinc. More than a dozen different flavonoid compounds in spinach function as anti-inflammatory and anti-cancer agents.[8,9,10]

INGREDIENTS:

Garlic sliced	3 cloves
Canola oil	4 t
Spinach baby or mature chopped	1 pound
Turmeric	¼ t
Salt	⅛ t
Black pepper, ground	⅛ t
Lemon juice	to taste or 1 T

DIRECTIONS:

1. Assemble and prepare all ingredients.
2. Add turmeric, salt, pepper and lemon juice to the spinach.
3. In a 3 to 4 quart pan heat sliced garlic for a minute on medium-high heat.
4. Quickly add oil and spinach with combined ingredients. Stir and cook on high for 2 minutes or just till spinach wilts.
5. Serve as a side dish with a meal containing grains and beans, such as with any khichadi (p. 94) and kadhi (p. 59), yogurt or raita (p. 49)

VARIATIONS & OPTIONS

- Substitute collard greens, swiss chard, bok choy or beet greens for spinach.

- Add cumin, mustard or fenugreek seeds with garlic.

- Add sliced jalapeño or ⅛ t cayenne pepper with spinach.

- Add thawed frozen green peas or corn with spinach.

- Add diced red, orange or yellow pepper with spinach.

- Add any cooked or canned beans with spinach; adjust seasonings.

- Add 1 T ground flax seeds with spinach.

NUTRITION INFORMATION PER SERVING:
Calories: 72 **Protein:** 3 g **Total Carbohydrates:** 5 g
Fiber: 3 g **Total Fat:** 5 g **Sodium:** 125 mg
Calcium: 117 mg **Omega-3 Fats (ALA):** 440 mg

Spinach with Split Mung Beans

Elaborate – Serves 6

Coriander seeds contain a variety of phytonutrients. They provide fiber and the minerals iron, magnesium and manganese. Cumin seeds provide manganese and iron as well as fiber.[8,9]

INGREDIENTS:

Split mung beans soaked in ½ Cup water	⅓ Cup
Water	⅓ Cup
Cumin seeds whole	½ t
Canola oil	2 T
Asafetida (hing)	pinch
Onion red, medium, chopped	1
Garlic chopped	4 cloves
Ginger fresh or frozen, grated	1 t
Tomato chopped	1
Turmeric	½ t
Salt	to taste or ¼ t
Cayenne pepper	⅛ t
Spinach baby or mature chopped	1 pound
Coriander-cumin powder (p. 132)	1 T

DIRECTIONS:

1. Assemble and prepare all ingredients.
2. Heat cumin seeds in a heavy bottomed 3-quart pan.
3. When cumin seeds are roasted add oil, asafetida and onion; sauté for 2 minutes till onion is tender.
4. Add garlic, ginger and tomato; cook for a minute.
5. Add soaked drained mung beans with ⅓-cup water, turmeric, salt and cayenne.
6. Stir to mix well; cook covered for 5 minutes.
7. Add spinach; cook till beans are tender and add coriander-cumin powder.
8. Serve as a side dish with a grain.

NUTRITION INFORMATION PER SERVING:
Calories: 104 **Protein:** 5 g **Total Carbohydrates:** 12 g
Fiber: 4 g **Total Fat:** 5 g **Sodium:** 111 mg
Calcium: 103 mg **Omega-3 Fats (ALA):** 440 mg

Green Beans
with Corn

Simple – Serves 6

Green beans supply a variety of carotenoids and flavonoids shown to have health-supportive antioxidant properties in addition to vitamins A, B1, B2, C, K, folate and niacin; as well as the minerals manganese, potassium, iron, magnesium, calcium, phosphorus and copper.[8,9,10]

INGREDIENTS:

Cumin seeds	¼ t
Black mustard seeds	¼ t
Canola oil	1 T
Asafetida (hing)	pinch
Green beans fresh or frozen cut	2 Cups
Corn fresh or thawed frozen	2 Cups
Milk low fat, dairy or non-dairy	1 Cup
Coconut dry unsweetened	2 T
Ginger fresh or frozen, grated	1 t
Garlic sliced	2 to 3 cloves
Jalapeño pepper cut in half	1
Turmeric	½ t
Salt	to taste or ¼ t
Cilantro fresh chopped with tender stems	½ Cup
Lemon or Lime juice	1 to 2 T

DIRECTIONS:

1. Assemble and prepare all ingredients.

2. Combine corn, beans, milk, coconut, ginger, garlic, jalapeño and turmeric; set aside.

3. Heat cumin and mustard seeds in a heavy-bottomed 3-quart pan.

4. Before the seeds pop add oil, asafetida and vegetables with combined ingredients.

5. Cook uncovered on high heat while stirring for 5 minutes, until most of the milk has been reduced.

6. Turn heat off and add salt, lemon or limejuice and cilantro; stir to mix.

7. Serve with a grain and bean dish as part of a meal.

   Note: Leftovers freeze well.

VARIATIONS & OPTIONS

- For non-dairy option use coconut, soy, almond or rice milk.

- You can also make this recipe without adding any milk. Cook covered in that case.

- Substitute any other vegetable for beans: peas, lima beans, cauliflower, spinach, mung bean sprouts, zucchini or edamame.

- Try these combinations:
  - Green beans with garlic or/ and ginger and cumin seeds.
  - Green beans with potato and mustard seeds.

NUTRITION INFORMATION PER SERVING:
Calories: 109 **Protein:** 4 g **Total Carbohydrates:** 17 g
Fiber: 3 g **Total Fat:** 4 g **Sodium:** 71 mg
Calcium: 70 mg **Omega-3 Fats (ALA):** 240 mg

Summer Squash

Simple – Serves 4

Summer squash, a fruit vegetable, contains the minerals manganese, magnesium, potassium, copper, phosphorus, calcium and zinc, as well as vitamins C, A, B1, B2, B6, folate and niacin.[8,9,10]

INGREDIENTS:

Cumin seeds . . . . ½ t
Canola oil . . . . 1 T
Garlic sliced . . . . .2 cloves
Zucchini or **yellow squash** cubed small . . . . .4 Cups
Turmeric . . . . ¼ t
Hot red or **black pepper** (or hot green chili, halved, 1) . . . . . . ¼ t
Salt . . . . ⅛ t
Cilantro chopped . . . . ¼ Cup
Lemon or **Limejuice** . . . . to taste

DIRECTIONS:

1. Assemble and prepare all ingredients.

2. Combine zucchini, pepper, salt and turmeric; set aside.

3. Heat a 2-quart pan or skillet and add cumin seeds.

4. When cumin seeds give off their aroma add oil and garlic.

5. When garlic is fried, a minute or less, add zucchini with combined ingredients.

6. Stir, cover and cook for a few minutes.

7. Before serving garnish with cilantro and a squirt of lemon or limejuice.

NUTRITION INFORMATION PER SERVING:
Calories: 59 **Protein:** 2 g **Total Carbohydrates:** 6 g
Fiber: 2 g **Total Fat:** 4 g **Sodium:** 44 mg
Calcium: 30 mg **Omega-3 Fats (ALA):** 360 mg

Mixed Vegetables (Undhiyu)

Simple – Serves 8

Using vegetables available here in the USA, I have adapted the traditional popular undhiyu eaten in the winter months in Gujarat.

INGREDIENTS:

Cilantro chopped with tender stems	2 Cups
Coconut unsweetened grated	¼ Cup
Ajwain	¾ t
Asafetida (hing)	a pinch
Salt	½ t
Garlic minced	1 t
Ginger fresh or frozen grated	1 t
Jalapeño or **hot green chili pepper** chopped	1
Turmeric	1 t
Olive oil	2 T
Potato cut into 1 ½" pieces	1 Cup
Onion medium cut into 1 ½" pieces	1
Eggplant cut into 1 ½" pieces	4 Cups
Sweet potato cut into 1 ½" pieces	1
Water	1 to 1½ Cups
Sugar snap peas, fresh or thawed if frozen	8 oz
Lima beans frozen, thawed	1 Cup
Lemon or **limejuice**	to taste

DIRECTIONS:

1. Assemble and prepare all ingredients.

2. In a heavy-bottomed 4-quart pan, mix together cilantro, coconut, ajwain, asafetida, salt, garlic, ginger, jalapeño, turmeric and oil.

3. Add the cut fresh vegetables and water; mix well.

4. Cook covered on medium high heat for 5 minutes, stir, and then turn heat down to medium; cook covered for 15 minutes.

5. Add lima beans and sugar snap peas, mix well; cook till potatoes are tender.

6. Before serving add lemon juice.

   Note: This is a good recipe that can be prepared and partially cooked the day before; add lima beans and peas on the day of serving. Leftovers keep well in the refrigerator for several days.

NUTRITION INFORMATION PER SERVING:
Calories: 129 **Protein:** 4 g **Total Carbohydrates:** 18 g
Fiber: 5 g **Total Fat:** 5 g **Sodium:** 138 mg
Calcium: 40 mg **Omega-3 Fats (ALA):** 30 mg

VARIATIONS & OPTIONS

- You can make this recipe without the ajwain, just omit it.

- Substitute chopped peanuts or sesame seeds for coconut.

- Substitute red chili pepper for jalapeño.

- Add carrots, turnips and/or beets to this recipe; adjust spices to taste.

- Reduce oil to reduce the total calories.

- Substitute 1½ – 2 cups of fresh cut tomatoes for the water.

- Substitute edamame for lima beans and make it a one-pot meal.

- Substitute fresh or frozen snow peas for the sugar snap peas.

www.FeedingHealth.com

Eggplant
Simple – Serves 4

Eggplants belong to the nightshade family of vegetables, which include tomatoes, sweet peppers and potatoes. Phytonutrients in eggplant include phenolic compounds and flavonoids, potent antioxidant and free radical scavengers shown to protect cell membranes from damage. Eggplant provides minerals such as potassium, manganese, copper and magnesium and B vitamins.[8,9,10]

INGREDIENTS:

Black mustard seeds	¼ t
Canola oil	1 T
Asafetida (hing)	pinch
Eggplant cut into big cubes	1
Water	¼ Cup
Turmeric	½ t
Salt	⅛ t
Red chili powder	¼ t
Sesame seeds or **sunflower seeds** or **coconut**	1 T
Cilantro chopped	for garnish
Lemon or **limejuice**	to taste

DIRECTIONS:

1. Assemble and prepare all ingredients.

2. Combine eggplant, water, turmeric and salt; set aside.

3. Heat a 2-quart pan and add mustard seeds.

4. Before the seeds begin to pop add oil, asafetida and combined ingredients.

5. Stir and cook covered for 5 minutes on medium heat.

6. Add sesame seeds and red chili powder; stir and cook covered till tender.

7. Add lemon or lime juice to taste, garnish with cilantro and serve as a side dish.

NUTRITION INFORMATION PER SERVING:
Calories: 75 **Protein:** 2 g **Total Carbohydrates:** 8 g
Fiber: 4 g **Total Fat:** 5 g **Sodium:** 40 mg
Calcium: 36 mg **Omega-3 Fats (ALA):** 360 mg

Eggplant with Onions and Tomatoes

Elaborate – Serves 8

Onions may help reduce cholesterol levels, blood pressure and blood sugar. Onion's antioxidants, such as quercetin, provide anti-inflammatory benefits.[8,9]

INGREDIENTS:

Black mustard seeds	½ t
Canola oil	3 T
Hot red peppers dried, whole	2
Asafetida (hing)	pinch
Onions red, medium, finely chopped	2
Garlic large cloves	3
Tomatoes medium, chopped	2
Ginger grated fresh or frozen	1 t
Eggplant large, cubed	1
Turmeric	½ t
Red pepper, cayenne, chili or **paprika**, ground	¼ t
Salt	½ t
Coriander-cumin powder (p. 132)	2 T
Cilantro fresh chopped with tender stems	½ Cup

DIRECTIONS:

1. Assemble and prepare all ingredients.
2. Heat a heavy bottomed 3-quart pan with mustard seeds.
3. Before the seeds begin to pop, add oil, asafetida, dry whole dry red peppers, garlic and onions. Sauté for a few minutes.
4. Add tomatoes, ginger, eggplant, turmeric, ground red pepper and salt.
5. Stir and cook till eggplant is tender. Turn heat off.
6. Add cilantro and coriander-cumin powder; stir to mix well.
7. Serve as a side dish with a meal containing rice, quinoa, khichadi (p. 94) or millet.

VARIATIONS & OPTIONS

- Eliminate whole dry red peppers if you do not have them or to decrease the heat.

- Substitute zucchini for the eggplant.

- Try a combination of eggplant, corn and cut zucchini in this recipe.

- Add ½ cup cooked or canned beans to this recipe.

- Use more tomatoes if you have extra in late summer and fall.

- Mash the eggplant after recipe is complete and use as a spread with pita bread or crackers.

- Substitute, or add, dark green leafy vegetable such as spinach, swiss chard or collard greens with the eggplant.

NUTRITION INFORMATION PER SERVING:
Calories: 91 **Protein:** 2 g **Total Carbohydrates:** 10 g
Fiber: 4 g **Total Fat:** 6 g **Sodium:** 76 mg
Calcium: 30 mg **Omega-3 Fats (ALA):** 500 mg

Kale

Simple – Serves 4

Kale contains vitamins A, C, B6 and K; minerals such as manganese, copper, calcium and potassium; as well as antioxidant phytonutrients and cancer-preventive nutrients. Sesame seeds provide some calcium and beneficial monounsaturated fats.[8,9,10]

INGREDIENTS:

Cumin seeds . . . . ½ t
Canola oil . . . . 1 T
Garlic sliced . . . . .1 clove
Sesame seeds . . . . 3 T
Kale coarsely chopped . . . . (1 bunch) 6 Cups
Water . . . . ½ to ¾ Cup
Salt . . . . ⅛ t
Turmeric . . . . ¼ t
Coriander-cumin powder (p. 132) . . . . .1 t
Lemon or **limejuice** . . . . to taste

DIRECTIONS:

1. Assemble and prepare all ingredients.
2. Heat the cumin seeds in a frying pan or pot over medium high heat.
3. When the seeds give off their aroma add oil, garlic, sesame seeds, kale, water and turmeric; stir.
4. Cook covered, on medium-high heat, till tender (about 10 minutes).
5. Stir and add salt to taste, coriander-cumin powder and lemon juice.
6. Serve as a side dish with a grain and bean or with khichadi (p. 94).

VARIATIONS & OPTIONS

- Substitute frozen kale for fresh if you are in a hurry.

- Substitute ground flax seeds for sesame seeds or use a combination of flax and sesame seeds. If using flax seeds add them with kale, not in the vaghar.

- Add diced tomatoes and reduce the amount of water.

- Substitute black mustard seeds for cumin seeds.

- Substitute any other dark green leafy vegetable (collard greens, swiss chard, spinach, or bok choy), fresh or frozen, for the kale.

- Substitute chopped onion for garlic in this recipe.

- Cook kale or other dark green leafy vegetable with corn or diced potato or even both together. Add potato to the vaghar first, cook covered for a few minutes; then add the greens and rest of the ingredients. If you increase the quantity of vegetables, increase oil and spices accordingly.

NUTRITION INFORMATION PER SERVING:
Calories: 125 Protein: 5 g Total Carbohydrates: 12 g
Fiber: 4 g Total Fat: 8 g Sodium: 83 mg
Calcium: 148 mg Omega-3 Fats (ALA): 520 mg

Kale as Crispy Chips

Simple – Serves 6

Lemons and limes provide unique phytonutrient properties as well as vitamin C, one of the most important antioxidants in nature. Lemon juice brings out the flavor in the kale chips.[8,9]

INGREDIENTS:

Oil spray canola or olive
Kale flat long-leaf, cut into 4" pieces . . . . 1 bunch
Salt . . . . ¼ t
Cayenne or **black pepper** . . . . ⅛ t
Lemon juice . . . . 1 T
Olive oil . . . . 2 T

DIRECTIONS:

1. Assemble and prepare all ingredients.

2. Preheat the oven to 400°F.

3. Coat two large baking sheets with oil spray.

4. Mix salt, cayenne or black pepper, lemon juice and olive oil well; coat the kale pieces front and back with this mixture.

5. Spread kale pieces into a single even layer between the two baking sheets.

6. Reduce oven temperature to 300°F. Bake 10 to 15 minutes or until kale is crispy to the touch and the edges are beginning to brown.

7. Enjoy these healthy and easy to make chips for a snack.

VARIATIONS & OPTIONS

- Add crushed garlic to the coating mixture.

- Add minced garlic and 2 T ground nuts, or peanut, almond or cashew butter, to the coating mixture.

- Use, in place of the coating mixture in the recipe, a combination of 2 T sesame tahini, 1 T fresh lemon or limejuice, 2 cloves minced fresh garlic and salt and pepper to taste.

Snow Peas with Garlic and Ginger

Simple – Serves 4

Green peas contain vitamins A, B1, B2, B6, folate, C, K and niacin; as well as the minerals manganese, phosphorus, magnesium, copper, iron, zinc and potassium.[8,9,10] Ginger is a good source of potassium, magnesium, copper, manganese and vitamin B6 in addition to providing anti-inflammatory effects.[8,9]

INGREDIENTS:

Cumin seeds	½ t
Canola oil	4 t
Hot green chili slit vertically into 4 pieces	1
Garlic crushed	3 cloves
Ginger fresh or frozen, grated	1 t
Snow peas	1 pound
Turmeric	½ t
Salt	to taste or ⅛ t
Cilantro with tender stems chopped	½ Cup
Lemon or **limejuice**	to taste

DIRECTIONS:

1. Assemble and prepare all ingredients.
2. Combine green chili, garlic, ginger, turmeric and peas; set aside.
3. Heat a heavy-bottomed 2-quart skillet or pan with cumin seeds.
4. When the seeds give off their aroma add oil and combined ingredients.
5. Stir and cook covered for 3 to 4 minutes.
6. Stir and cook uncovered for a few more minutes till crisp tender.
7. Add salt to taste, lemon or limejuice and cilantro before serving as a side dish.

VARIATIONS & OPTIONS

- Substitute either green peas or sugar snap peas for the snow peas.
- Use either garlic or ginger instead of using both.
- Use hot red or black pepper powder in place of the green chilies.
- If you have colored peppers, slice them and cook with the peas.
- Substitute diced zucchini, lima beans or edamame with corn for the peas.
- Substitute thinly sliced white potato for the peas in this recipe.
- Substitute fresh baby spinach for the peas or add some with the peas.

NUTRITION INFORMATION PER SERVING:
Calories: 94 **Protein:** 6 g **Total Carbohydrates:** 11 g
Fiber: 3 g **Total Fat:** 5 g **Sodium:** 51 mg
Calcium: 66 mg **Omega-3 Fats (ALA):** 440 mg

Peas with Tofu
Elaborate – Serves 8

Tomatoes provide vitamins A, B1, B2, B6, C, K, E, folate, pantothenic acid and niacin; minerals such as molybdenum, potassium, manganese, chromium, copper, magnesium, iron and phosphorus as well as lycopene.[8,9,10]

INGREDIENTS:

Cumin seeds. . . . . .1 t
Canola oil for sautéing onions. 1 T
Canola oil for preparing tofu. . . . . .1 t
Onion red, medium, finely chopped 1
Ginger, grated . . . . .1 t
Garlic minced . . . . .1 t
Hot red pepper ground . . . . ½ t
Turmeric. . . . . .1 t
Coriander-cumin powder (p. 132). . . . . 1 T
Tomato purée or **tomato juice** .2 Cups
Green peas fresh or frozen. . . . . .1 pound
Salt. . . . . ¼ t
Tofu firm, drained, cubed. . . . . ½ pound
Cilantro with tender stems chopped . . . . 1 Cup

DIRECTIONS:

1. Assemble and prepare all ingredients; preheat oven to 400°F.

2. Combine garlic, ginger, turmeric, red pepper, coriander-cumin powder and tomato juice or tomato puree; set aside.

3. Put tofu cubes between paper towels or dishtowels to draw off some of the water.

4. Toss tofu cubes gently with 1 t oil; bake coated tofu cubes at 400°F for 20 minutes. Remove from oven and set aside.

5. Heat a 3-quart skillet or pan with cumin seeds. When the seeds give off their aroma add oil and chopped onion.

6. Sauté till onion is tender; add combined ingredients and cook for 5 – 7 minutes.

7. Add green peas, salt and baked tofu cubes.

8. Cook till peas are tender, a few minutes if using frozen peas, longer if using fresh peas.

9. Turn heat off, add cilantro; stir to mix and serve with a grain.

VARIATIONS & OPTIONS

- Substitute potatoes, eggplant, zucchini or cauliflower for tofu.

- Substitute cooked chickpeas or any other cooked beans for tofu.

- Substitute fresh-cut tomatoes when you have them in the summer (and cook a little longer) or use tomato paste with water if you don't have tomato juice or purée.

NUTRITION INFORMATION PER SERVING:
Calories: 142 **Protein:** 9 g **Total Carbohydrates:** 17 g
Fiber: 5 g **Total Fat:** 5 g **Sodium:** 294 mg
Calcium: 233 mg **Omega-3 Fats (ALA):** 220 mg

Root Vegetables Stir-fried: Sweet, Sour and Mildly Hot

Simple – Serves 8

Roots, bulbs, and tubers have higher starch content than other vegetables and are good sources of vitamin C and potassium. Sweet potatoes and carrots also provide beta-carotene while onions and garlic, research suggests, may lower blood pressure and cholesterol. Root vegetables, especially sweet potatoes, create a favorable alkaline environment in the body.[8,9,10]

INGREDIENTS:

Cumin seeds	¼ t
Black mustard seeds	¼ t
Canola oil	2 T
Asafetida (hing)	pinch
Onion red, large chopped	1
Jalapeño pepper cut in half	1
White sweet potato peeled, cubed	2 Cups
White potato cubed	2 Cups
Turnip peeled, cubed	2 Cups
Water	⅓ Cup
Turmeric	½ t
Salt	¼ t
Cilantro chopped with tender stems	1 Cup
Lemon or **limejuice**	one-half

DIRECTIONS:

1. Assemble and prepare all ingredients.

2. Combine cut vegetables, water, salt and turmeric.

3. Heat a heavy-bottomed 3-quart pan on medium-high with cumin and mustard seeds.

4. Before seeds start to pop add oil, asafetida, onion and jalapeño; sauté 1-2 minutes.

5. Add vegetables with combined ingredients; stir and cook till tender.

6. Add cilantro and lemon or limejuice before serving as a starch with a meal.

NUTRITION INFORMATION PER SERVING:

Calories: 107 **Protein:** 2 g **Total Carbohydrates:** 18 g
Fiber: 2.5 g **Total Fat:** 3.5 g **Sodium:** 79 mg
Calcium: 31 mg **Omega-3 Fats (ALA):** 350 mg

Potatoes with Garlic, Stir-fried

Simple – Serves 6

Potatoes provide vitamins C and B6, as well as the minerals copper, potassium and manganese.[8] Garlic contains sulfur molecules many of which are shown to function as antioxidants with anti-inflammatory properties. Garlic supplies the minerals manganese, phosphorus, selenium, calcium, potassium and copper; and vitamins B1, B6 and C.[8,9,10]

INGREDIENTS:

Cumin seeds	½ t
Canola oil	4 t
Asafetida (hing)	pinch
Potatoes white, cubed small	4 Cups
Water	¼ Cup
Garlic sliced	3 cloves
Sesame seeds or **chopped peanuts**	2 T
Turmeric	½ t
Salt	to taste or ¼ t
Cayenne pepper	¼ t
Lemon or **lime juiced**	½
Cilantro chopped with tender stems	½ Cup

DIRECTIONS:

1. Assemble and prepare all ingredients.

2. Combine cut potatoes, water, turmeric, sesame seeds and garlic; set aside.

3. Heat on medium-high a heavy-bottomed 2-quart pan with cumin seeds.

4. When the seeds give off their aroma add oil, asafetida and potatoes with combined ingredients. Turn heat to medium; add salt and cayenne; stir and cook covered for 5 to 7 minutes; stirring occasionally until potatoes are tender.

5. Before serving as a side dish add lemon or limejuice and cilantro.

VARIATIONS & OPTIONS

- Just before serving stir in some plain yogurt in this recipe.

- Substitute sliced onion for garlic; when potatoes are tender stir in 1 T coriander-cumin powder (p. 132).

- Add onion, diced tomato and green peas to the potatoes. Adjust spices for the additional vegetables.

- Add 1 T of ground flax seeds with the cilantro and lemon or limejuice.

- Add spinach or any other dark green leafy vegetable to the potatoes and adjust salt and cayenne accordingly.

- Substitute mustard and fenugreek seeds for cumin seeds.

NUTRITION INFORMATION PER SERVING:

Calories: 127 **Protein:** 3 g **Total Carbohydrates:** 19 g
Fiber: 3 g **Total Fat:** 5 g **Sodium:** 55 mg
Calcium: 20 mg **Omega-3 Fats (ALA):** 300 mg

Potatoes in Yogurt Sauce

Elaborate – Serves 8

Cloves have a variety of phytonutrients and contain a volatile oil that can be up to 90% eugenol, which inhibits platelet activity and functions as an anti-inflammatory.[8,9]

INGREDIENTS:

Black mustard seeds	¼ t
Canola oil	2 T
Cloves whole	3
Asafetida (hing)	pinch
Chickpea flour (besan)	3 T
Yogurt plain low fat	1½ Cups
Water	1 Cup
Salt	¼ t
Ginger grated	1 t
Jalapeño chopped	one-half
Turmeric	½ t
Potatoes partially boiled, cubed	4 Cups
Cilantro chopped with tender stems	½ to 1 Cup

DIRECTIONS:

1. Assemble and prepare all ingredients.

2. Combine yogurt, water, salt, ginger, jalapeño and turmeric; set aside.

3. Heat a heavy-bottomed 2-quart pot on medium-high with mustard seeds. Before the seeds begin to pop turn heat off with pot on the burner.

4. Add oil, asafetida, cloves and chickpea flour. Roast the flour for a minute or two until its color deepens.

5. Add yogurt with combined ingredients and cubed potatoes; stir to mix well; cook covered on medium heat till the mixture comes to a boil and potatoes are tender; stirring once or twice.

6. Add cilantro before serving with a khichadi (p. 94) or any grain.

VARIATIONS & OPTIONS

- Add either garlic or onion before adding the chickpea flour in the vaghar in step 4. If adding onion, do not turn heat off. Once the onion is tender add the chickpea flour and follow the recipe.

- Substitute ¼ cup chopped mint leaves for the cilantro.

- Substitute 1 ½ to 2 cups cooked mung beans, chickpeas or kidney beans for potatoes.

- Add green peas, chopped tomato or diced sweet bell peppers to this dish.

- Add steamed broccoli or steamed Brussels sprouts to the yogurt sauce once it is cooked. In step 5 of this recipe, allow the yogurt mixture to come to a boil; then add steamed broccoli or steamed Brussels sprouts instead of the potatoes.

- If you cook just the sauce without adding the potatoes, the sauce can be frozen for use at another meal.

NUTRITION INFORMATION PER SERVING:
Calories: 127 **Protein:** 4 g **Total Carbohydrates:** 18 g
Fiber: 2 g **Total Fat:** 4 g **Sodium:** 78 mg
Calcium: 88 mg **Omega-3 Fats (ALA):** 330 mg

Okra Stir-fried

Simple – Serves 6

Okra is a fruit vegetable that contains vitamins C, B, folic acid; phytonutrients and minerals such as magnesium, potassium and calcium. Almost 30% of okra's calories come from protein.[8,9,10]

INGREDIENTS:

Black mustard seeds	½ t
Cumin seeds	1 t
Fenugreek seeds	1½ t
Canola oil	2 T
Asafetida (hing)	pinch
Okra sliced ¾" to 1"	6 Cups
Turmeric	1 t
Sesame seeds	2 T
Coconut dried, unsweetened, grated	1 T
Salt	to taste or ¼ t
Cayenne pepper	¼ t
Cilantro chopped with tender stems	½ c
Lemon or **limejuice**	to taste

DIRECTIONS:

1. Assemble and prepare all ingredients.

2. Heat on high a heavy-bottomed 2-quart skillet with mustard, cumin and fenugreek seeds.

3. Before the seeds begin to pop add oil, asafetida and okra. Reduce heat to medium and stir.

4. Add turmeric, sesame seeds and coconut; stir to mix. Cook covered on medium to medium-low heat for 10 minutes stirring 2 to 3 times.

5. Add salt and cayenne; stir to mix and cook uncovered until okra is tender.

6. Before serving garnish with cilantro and lime or lemon juice.

7. Serve as a side dish with a meal or with a khichadi (p. 94).

8. Leftovers freeze well and can be refrigerated for several days.

   Note: Okra can absorb a lot of oil, however, I have used less oil. Adding more oil will make the okra crisper and drier if that is what you are looking for.

VARIATIONS & OPTIONS

- Substitute ¼ cup of chopped or crushed peanuts for coconut and sesame seeds.

- Use less oil if you prefer and bake the okra in the oven
  - Dry-roast ¼ cup of chickpea flour in a skillet on medium heat till color deepens slightly. Remove from heat promptly to prevent burning the flour.
  - Mix the dry-roasted chickpea flour, ¼ cup of chopped peanuts (or sesame seeds or coconut), 1 t ground cumin, ¼ to ½ t cayenne pepper, 1 t crushed garlic, 1 ½ cup chopped cilantro, ½ t salt and 1 ½ t turmeric.
  - Proceed with steps 1 through 3 of the recipe and remove from heat.
  - Add the chickpea flour mixture to the okra, mix well and bake covered in the oven at 350°F for 30 minutes or till the okra is tender. Bake uncovered for 5 more minutes after okra is tender.
  - Garnish with fresh cilantro and add lemon or lime juice to taste.

- For okra in yogurt sauce:
  - Mix 2 cups plain yogurt with 1 cup water, ¼ t salt, 1 t grated ginger, ½ chopped jalapeño, ½ t turmeric and set aside. Measure 3 T chickpea flour; set aside.
  - Proceed with steps 1 to 2 of the original recipe.
  - Before the seeds begin to pop add 2–3 T oil, asafetida and 3 T chickpea flour. With heat off roast the flour for a minute or two until color deepens.
  - Add the yogurt mixture and stir it into the flour to mix well; turn heat on to medium-to-medium high.
  - Add the prepared okra and cook, stirring in between, till okra is tender.
  - Garnish with chopped cilantro and cut tomatoes.

NUTRITION INFORMATION PER SERVING:
Calories: 103 **Protein:** 3 g **Total Carbohydrates:** 9 g
Fiber: 4 g **Total Fat:** 7 g **Sodium:** 58 mg
Calcium: 91mg **Omega-3 Fats (ALA):** 450 mg

Broccoli

Simple – Serves 4

Broccoli contains sulforaphane, isothiocyanate and indoles, phytonutrients that enhance the breakdown and excretion of cancer-causing compounds in the liver. Broccoli also provides vitamins B, C, K, E and folate; carotenoids and minerals such as manganese, potassium, magnesium, phosphorus, iron, calcium and zinc.[5,8,9,10]

INGREDIENTS:

Broccoli cut . . . . 4 Cups
Lemon or **limejuice** . . . . to taste
Salt . . . . to taste
Black pepper . . . . to taste

DIRECTIONS:

1. Assemble and prepare all ingredients.
2. Steam the broccoli for a few minutes, until crisp-tender.
3. Add salt, pepper and lemon or limejuice to taste.

VARIATIONS & OPTIONS

- Top steamed broccoli with sesame tahini sauce (p. 63)

- Top steamed broccoli with a plain carrot or cucumber raita (p. 49)

- Stir-fry, roast or steam broccoli with fresh or frozen corn.

Broccoli

Elaborate – Serves 4

INGREDIENTS:

Broccoli cut in small pieces . . . . 4 Cups
Black mustard seeds . . . . ¼ t
Canola oil . . . . 1 T
Asafetida (hing) . . . . pinch
Chickpea flour . . . . 1 T
Yogurt low fat, plain (or water). . . . . ¼ Cup
Turmeric. . . . . ¼ t
Cayenne pepper. . . . . ⅛ t
Salt . . . . a sprinkle, to taste
Lemon or **limejuice**. . . . . to taste

DIRECTIONS:

1. Assemble and prepare all ingredients.
2. Combine turmeric, salt and cayenne with yogurt or water.
3. Heat mustard seeds in a pan. Before the seeds begin to pop, turn heat off and add oil, asafetida and chickpea flour.
4. Stir with heat off to toast the chickpea flour in the hot pan for a few minutes.
5. Add the yogurt or water mixture, stir and turn heat to medium. Cook covered for 5 minutes to bring this to a boil.
6. Add broccoli and stir to mix ingredients. Cook covered 5 to 6 minutes or till broccoli is crisp-tender or until desired texture.
7. Before serving add lime or lemon juice to taste.

NUTRITION INFORMATION PER SERVING:
Calories: 81 **Protein:** 4 g **Total Carbohydrates:** 9 g
Fiber: 4 g **Total Fat:** 4 g **Sodium:** 113 mg
Calcium: 71 mg **Omega-3 Fats (ALA):** 350 mg

Asparagus

Simple – Serves 4

Asparagus, a member of the lily family, provides over 50% of its calories from protein in addition to providing flavonoids, antioxidants, vitamins K, C, A, B1, B2, B3, B6 and folate; and minerals such as manganese, copper, phosphorus and potassium. Asparagus helps maintain a more alkaline environment in the body.[8,9,10]

INGREDIENTS:

Asparagus trimmed	¾ pound
Water	2 T
Olive oil	2 t
Turmeric	½ t
Salt	⅛ t
Black pepper	to taste
Lemon juice	to taste

DIRECTIONS:

1. Assemble and prepare all ingredients.
2. Heat a heavy-bottom pan on high. Add asparagus, water, oil, turmeric and salt.
3. Stir-fry to mix the ingredients, cover and cook on medium high heat for 2 to 3 minutes or until crisp-tender.
4. Add pepper and lemon juice to taste and serve.

Asparagus

Elaborate – Serves 4

INGREDIENTS:

Asparagus trimmed, tips cut 3", tender stems cut 1"	¾ pound
Turmeric	½ t
Salt	⅛ t
Sesame seeds	2 T
Cumin Seeds	½ t
Olive oil	1 T
Garlic sliced	1 clove
Hot green pepper sliced	one-half
Water	2 T
Cilantro chopped	to taste or ¼ Cup
Lemon juice	1 T

DIRECTIONS:

1. Assemble and prepare all ingredients.
2. Add turmeric, salt and sesame seeds to the cut asparagus.
3. Heat cumin seeds in a skillet on medium high till they are toasted.
4. Add oil, garlic and hot pepper to cumin seeds.
5. Add cut asparagus with combined ingredients and water; stir and cook covered on medium high heat 2 to 3 minutes or until crisp-tender. Stir, remove from heat and discard hot pepper.
6. Add cilantro and lemon juice to taste and serve as a side dish.

NUTRITION INFORMATION PER SERVING:

Calories: 79 **Protein:** 3 g **Total Carbohydrates:** 6 g
Fiber: 2.5 g **Total Fat:** 6 g **Sodium:** 39 mg
Calcium: 71 mg **Omega-3 Fats (ALA):** 50 mg

VARIATIONS & OPTIONS

- Sprinkle the asparagus with olive oil, minced garlic and turmeric and roast in a 375°F oven for 15 to 20 minutes. Add salt, pepper, lemon juice or balsamic vinegar to taste.

- Stir-fry thin-sliced shallots in oil; now add asparagus, turmeric and water; stir-fry until crisp-tender. Season and serve.

- Substitute broccoli for the asparagus.

- Top steamed asparagus with sesame tahini sauce (p. 63) in place of oil, salt, pepper and lemon.

- Roast asparagus with fresh or frozen corn.

- Add cut asparagus to cubed and almost cooked potatoes.

- Combine asparagus with cooked quinoa, rice or barley.

Brussels Sprouts Roasted

Simple – Serves 6

Brussels sprouts contain sulforaphane, isothiocyanate and indoles, phytonutrients that enhance the breakdown and excretion of cancer-causing compounds in the liver; as well as vitamins C, K, A, B1, B2, B6, folate and E; and minerals including manganese, potassium, iron, phosphorus, magnesium, copper and calcium.[5,8,9,10]

INGREDIENTS:

Brussels Sprouts	1½ pounds
Garlic peeled and sliced	3 to 4 cloves
Olive Oil	2 T
Salt	to taste or ¼ t
Turmeric	½ teaspoon
Black Pepper freshly ground	to taste
Lime or **Lemon** or **Balsamic Vinegar**	to taste

DIRECTIONS:

1. Preheat the oven to 500°F and assemble and prepare all ingredients.

2. Soak the Brussels sprouts in a bowl of warm water for 5 to 10 minutes to eliminate any insects hidden in the leaves. Rinse the sprouts in fresh water.

3. Trim the stem ends of the sprouts not quite flush with the bottoms (so the outer leaves don't fall off during cooking). Unless they are very small and tender, cut the sprouts in half vertically.

4. Combine sprouts, garlic, oil, salt and turmeric. Mix well.

5. Place dressed sprouts in an ovenproof dish and roast uncovered for 5 minutes at 500°F.

6. Reduce the heat to 375°F and roast for another 15 minutes until the sprouts are just tender.

7. Turn oven off; cover the sprouts and leave them in the oven another 5 to 10 minutes until you are ready to eat. After 10 minutes take them out of the oven to prevent overcooking.

8. Before serving add lemon or limejuice or balsamic vinegar. Serve with a meal.

VARIATIONS & OPTIONS

- Roasting is my favorite way to cook Brussels sprouts but you can also boil, braise or steam them.

- Top roasted Brussels sprouts with sesame tahini sauce (p. 63) or put roasted or steamed Brussels sprouts in kadhi (p. 59) or add to any raita (p. 49).

- Sprinkle 1 T of ground flax seeds on the roasted Brussels sprouts.

- Roast Brussels sprouts with fresh corn kernels.

- Substitute asparagus, beets, green beans, cauliflower, broccoli, snow peas, sugar snap peas or root vegetables for Brussels sprouts. The cooking times will vary.

NUTRITION INFORMATION PER SERVING:
Calories: 93 **Protein:** 4 g **Total Carbohydrates:** 11 g
Fiber: 4 g **Total Fat:** 5 g **Sodium:** 29 mg
Calcium: 51 mg **Omega-3 Fats (ALA):** 150 mg

Salads

Cabbage Salad,
Green and Red

Simple – Serves 6

Cabbage contains sulforaphane, isothiocyanate and indoles, phytochemicals that enhance the breakdown and excretion of cancer-causing compounds in the liver; vitamins C, K, A, B, folate; as well as the minerals manganese, potassium, calcium and magnesium.[8,9,10] Red cabbage provides significantly more protective phytonutrients than green cabbage. The color of red cabbage reflects its concentration of anthocyanin polyphenols, which provide antioxidants, are anti-inflammatory and promote health.[8,9]

INGREDIENTS:

Black mustard seeds	½ t
Olive oil	2 T
Asafetida	pinch
Red cabbage finely shredded	4 Cups
Green cabbage finely shredded	4 Cups
Hot green chili pepper sliced	1
Salt	⅛ t
Turmeric	½ t
Cilantro chopped with tender stems	1 Cup
Lemon or **limejuice**	1 T

DIRECTIONS:

1. Assemble and prepare all ingredients.

2. Combine sliced green chili, salt, turmeric and shredded cabbage; set aside.

3. Heat a heavy-bottomed 3-quart pan with mustard seeds. Before the seeds begin to pop add oil, asafetida and combined ingredients. Stir to mix; cook on medium-high heat for 3 to 4 minutes. Turn heat off.

4. Before serving add cilantro and lemon juice; mix well.

5. If you like the cabbage less crisp, cook it for a longer time.

VARIATIONS & OPTIONS

- If you prefer to eat this raw, then make a dressing of 1 to 1 ½ cups plain low fat yogurt, ⅛ t salt or to taste, ½ t fresh ground black or red chili pepper, 1 t ground cumin powder, ¼ t lemon zest, and 1 T lemon juice. Add 2 T chopped fresh dill leaves to the yogurt dressing and omit cilantro if you prefer. I like cilantro and dill together. Toss the 8 cups cabbage and 1 cup cilantro with this dressing.

- Substitute napa or savoy cabbage for green cabbage.

- Add cooked or canned beans to the cabbage salad.

- Substitute parsley for cilantro.

NUTRITION INFORMATION PER SERVING:
Calories: 70 **Protein:** 2 g **Total carbohydrates:** 6 g
Fiber: 2.5 g **Total fat:** 5 g **Sodium:** 42 mg
Calcium: 49 mg **Omega-3 Fats (ALA):** 470 mg

Papaya Salad

Simple – Serves 6

Papaya supplies vitamins C, E, A, K and folate; potassium, phytonutrients and fiber.[8,9,10] *Asafetida (also known as hing) is a resin with a strong aroma and is available in Indian grocery stores. Although used in very small quantities it imparts a flavor to the food.*

INGREDIENTS:

Black mustard seeds . . . . ¼ t
Olive oil . . . . 2 T
Asafetida . . . . .a pinch
Papaya under ripe, peeled, grated . . . . .4 Cups
Salt . . . . ⅛ t
Ginger fresh, grated . . . . ½ t
Hot green chili pepper finely minced . . . . ½ t
Lemon or **limejuice** . . . . one-half
Cilantro chopped with tender stems . . . . ⅓ Cup

DIRECTIONS:

1. Assemble and prepare all ingredients.
2. Combine papaya, salt, ginger and hot chili pepper.
3. Heat a 2-quart pan with mustard seeds; before the seeds pop add oil, asafetida and papaya mixture.
4. Stir fry quickly for a few minutes. Turn heat off.
5. Add lemon or lime and cilantro; stir to mix well.
6. Serve as a side dish with lunch or dinner meal or use as a filling in a wrap or pita pocket.

VARIATIONS & OPTIONS

- Substitute grated carrots for papaya or add some to the grated papaya.

- Substitute a combination of shredded cabbage and grated carrots for papaya.

- Use a combination of diced under ripe mango with under ripe papaya.

- Substitute colored sweet peppers diced small for grated papaya.

- If you do not have either ginger or hot green chili, you can still make this salad. Simply omit either or both or replace them with ground black or red pepper.

- You can make this without asafetida if you prefer.

NUTRITION INFORMATION PER SERVING:
Calories: 102 **Protein:** 1 gram **Total carbohydrates:** 15 g
Fiber: 3 g **Total fat:** 5 g **Sodium:** 29 mg
Calcium: 39 mg **Omega-3 Fats (ALA):** 80 mg

Cucumber Salad
Simple – Serves 4

Cucumbers supply vitamins C, A and folate; minerals molybdenum, potassium, manganese, magnesium and silica in addition to fiber. Cilantro has been shown to lower blood sugar in animals. In parts of India it has traditionally been used as an anti-inflammatory agent. Coriander's exceptional phytonutrient content, flavonoids and active phenolic acid compounds contribute to its healing properties. According to Ayurveda coriander is cooling and aids digestion.[8,9]

INGREDIENTS:

English cucumber cut small	4 Cups
Peanuts chopped	¼ Cup
Cilantro chopped with tender stems	½ Cup
Cumin ground	½ t
Salt	just a dash to taste
Red or **black pepper** ground	to taste
Lime juiced	one-half

DIRECTIONS:

1. Assemble and prepare all ingredients.
2. Mix all the ingredients together.
3. Enjoy as a side dish with a meal.

VARIATIONS & OPTIONS

- Add a little fresh grated ginger and finely minced hot green chili pepper.

- Add a little lemon zest to the salad.

- Combine grated carrots with grated cucumber for added color, texture and taste.

- Add fresh chives to the salad.

- Add grape or cherry tomatoes or red and/or green grapes to the salad.

NUTRITION INFORMATION PER SERVING:
Calories: 67 **Protein:** 3 g **Total carbohydrates:** 5 g
Fiber: 1.5 g **Total fat:** 4 g **Sodium:** 40 mg
Calcium: 31 mg **Omega-3 Fats (ALA):** 0 mg

Mixed Vegetables Salad

Simple – Serves 4

Herbs and spices, in use since approximately 5,000 B.C.E., are among the richest sources of antioxidants. Cumin, both seeds and powder, may have hypoglycemic effects. According to Ayurveda cumin seeds aid digestion and balance all three doshas. Tomatoes provide vitamins A, B1, B2, B6, C, K, E, folate, pantothenic acid and niacin; minerals such as molybdenum, potassium, manganese, chromium, copper, magnesium, iron and phosphorus as well as lycopene. [8,9,10]

INGREDIENTS:

Cucumber cut small	1
Carrots grated	1 Cup
Tomatoes chopped	1 Cup
Scallions chopped	1 Cup
Salt	⅛ t
Cumin powder	½ to 1 t
Black pepper freshly ground	to taste
Herb, choice of **cilantro**, **parsley**, **basil** or **mint** chopped	to taste
Lime or **lemon** juiced	one-half

DIRECTIONS:

1. Assemble and prepare all ingredients.
2. Combine the vegetables with herbs, salt, cumin, lime or lemon juice and black pepper.
3. Serve with a meal or as a filling in a wrap or pita pocket.

VARIATIONS & OPTIONS

- Substitute 1 cup grated beet root for part of the vegetables in this recipe.

- Substitute ¼ cup finely chopped sweet vidalia onion for 1 cup scallions.

- Add steamed edamame, lima beans, cooked chickpeas or peas to this salad.

- Add 3 T chopped nuts, grated coconut or ground flax or sesame seeds to the salad.

- Add 2 T raisins and 2 T Greek yogurt to the salad.

- Add lentil, mung bean or soy sprouts to the salad.

NUTRITION INFORMATION PER SERVING:
Calories: 39 **Protein:** 2 g **Total carbohydrates:** 9 g
Fiber: 2 g **Total fat:** 0 g **Sodium:** 63 mg
Calcium: 45 mg **Omega-3 Fats (ALA):** 0 mg

Onions Marinated

Simple – Serves 6

Onions contain vitamins B6, C and folate; as well as the minerals chromium, manganese, molybdenum, potassium, phosphorus and copper. They are low in calories and have high polyphenol content and a large amount of quercetin. The flavonoids in onion are concentrated in the outer layers of the flesh. Peel off as little of the fleshy, edible portion as possible when removing the onion's outermost paper layer. Even a small amount of "over peeling" can result in loss of flavonoids. For example, a red onion can lose about 20% of its quercetin and almost 75% of its anthocyanins if it is "over peeled."[8,9,10]

INGREDIENTS:

Red onions thinly sliced . . . . .1 ½ Cups
Salt. . . . . ⅛ t
Lime or **lemon** juiced. . . . . 3 to 4 T
Paprika. . . . . to taste or 1 to 2 t
Cumin ground . . . . .1 t
Sugar . . . . .1 t
Cilantro fresh, chopped . . . . ½ Cup

DIRECTIONS:

1. Assemble and prepare all ingredients.

2. Combine sliced onions, salt, lime or lemon juice, paprika, ground cumin, sugar and chopped herbs. Mix together.

3. Allow the salad to marinate chilled or at room temperature for a couple of hours before eating.

4. Serve as a condiment with a meal.

5. Leftovers keep in the refrigerator for 4-5 days.

VARIATIONS & OPTIONS

- Add a little grated fresh ginger with the onions.

- Substitute sweet vidalia onion for red onion.

- Substitute 2 T of fresh chopped mint for cilantro.

NUTRITION INFORMATION PER SERVING:
Calories: 21 **Protein:** 0 g **Total carbohydrates:** 5 g
Fiber: 1 gram **Total fat:** 0 g **Sodium:** 26 mg
Calcium: 12 mg **Omega-3 Fats (ALA):** 10 mg

RAITA

Rai means mustard seeds, so traditionally raita is coarsely ground black mustard seeds in plain yogurt. With creativity, you can add just about anything to yogurt to make a raita. A raita can be served with most vegetarian meals. Vegan cooks can use plain soy yogurt to make raita, or try a combination of whipped silken tofu and soy yogurt. Make banana raita with ripe bananas. Raita can be made using grated radishes, raisins, cooked potatoes (it resembles a potato salad), roasted eggplant, spinach, coconut, cilantro, cooked okra, cucumbers, carrots, tomatoes and mushrooms. Here are a few examples to get you started making raita:

Raita with Radish
Simple – Serves 4

Radishes are root vegetables with a distinctive flavor ranging from mild to sharp, depending on the variety. One cup of sliced radishes provides 30% of the daily vitamin C requirement with less than 25 calories.[8,9,10] Adding them to yogurt is one way my mother enjoyed her radishes.

INGREDIENTS:
Radishes trimmed, grated . . . . 1 Cup
Yogurt low fat, dairy or non-dairy, plain. . . . . ½ Cup
Salt. . . . . .a sprinkle or to taste
Black mustard seeds ground. . . . . ¼ t
Cilantro with tender stems, chopped . . . . 2 T

DIRECTIONS:
1. Assemble and prepare all ingredients.
2. Combine yogurt, salt, mustard, grated radishes and cilantro. Mix well.
3. Serve as a side dish or condiment with a meal.

VARIATIONS & OPTIONS
- Substitute grated turnips, carrots or beets for the radishes.
- Substitute a combination of radish and leftover cooked potatoes.
- Substitute a combination of radish and cucumber.

NUTRITION INFORMATION PER SERVING:
Calories: 24 **Protein:** 2 g **Total carbohydrates:** 3 g
Fiber: 0.5 g **Total fat:** 0.5 g **Sodium:** 70 mg
Calcium: 59 mg **Omega-3 Fats (ALA):** 10 mg

Raita with Banana

Simple – Serves 6

Bananas provide vitamins B6 and C, the minerals potassium and manganese as well as fiber. Mustard seeds and powder, like other Brassicas, contain plenty of phytonutrients. Isothiocyanates in mustard seed and other Brassicas have been repeatedly studied for their anti-cancer effects.[8,9]

INGREDIENTS:

Bananas ripe, mashed 2
Yogurt low fat, dairy or non-dairy, plain. . . . . 1 Cup
Black mustard seeds coarsely ground . . . . ¼ to ½ t
Salt . . . . a dash to taste

DIRECTIONS:

1. Assemble and prepare all ingredients.
2. Combine all the ingredients; mix well.
3. Chill if desired and serve with a meal.

NUTRITION INFORMATION PER SERVING:
Calories: 61 **Protein:** 2 g **Total carbohydrates:** 12 g
Fiber: 1 gram **Total fat:** 0.5 g **Sodium:** 55 mg
Calcium: 69 mg **Omega-3 Fats (ALA):** 10 mg

Raita with Cucumber

Simple – Serves 6

Cucumber provides vitamins C, A and folate; and the minerals molybdenum, potassium, manganese, magnesium and silica as well as fiber. Ginger is a good source of potassium, magnesium, copper, manganese and vitamin B6 in addition to providing anti-inflammatory effects.[8,9]

INGREDIENTS:

Raisins . . . . 2 T
Hot green chili pepper minced . . . . to taste or ½ t
Ginger fresh or frozen grated . . . . ½ t
Salt . . . . to taste or ⅛ t
Black mustard seeds coarsely ground . . . . ½ t
Yogurt low fat, dairy or non-dairy, plain. . . . . 1 Cup
Cucumber grated . . . . .2 Cups

DIRECTIONS:

1. Assemble and prepare all ingredients.

2. Combine all the ingredients together; mix well.

3. Serve with a meal.

VARIATIONS & OPTIONS

- Substitute greek yogurt for regular yogurt.

- Substitute grated carrots or chopped tomato for grated cucumber.

- Try a combination of grated carrots or chopped tomato with grated cucumber.

- Substitute fresh coarsely ground black pepper to taste for hot green chili.

- Add 2 T sunflower seeds or chopped nuts.

- Add chopped fresh cilantro to the raita.

- Add 1 to 2 T of finely chopped onion, chives or scallion to the raita.

NUTRITION INFORMATION PER SERVING:
Calories: 40 **Protein:** 2 g **Total carbohydrates:** 6 g
Fiber: 0.5 g **Total fat:** 0.5 g **Sodium:** 56 mg
Calcium: 75 mg **Omega-3 Fats (ALA):** 10 mg

Raita with Carrot

Simple – Serves 8

Carrots contain beta-carotene, which protects vision, especially night vision. Beta-carotene's powerful antioxidant actions help provide protection against macular degeneration and the development of senile cataracts which are the leading cause of blindness in the elderly.[8,9]

INGREDIENTS:

Carrots grated . . . . 4 Cups
Cilantro chopped with tender stems . . . . ½ Cup
Hot green pepper minced . . . . ½ t
Peanuts coarsely chopped . . . . ¼ Cup
Raisins . . . . ¼ Cup
Salt . . . . to taste or ⅛ t
Cumin ground . . . . 1 t
Yogurt low fat, dairy or non-dairy, plain . . . . 1½ Cups

DIRECTIONS:

1. Assemble and prepare all ingredients.
2. Mix all the ingredients together; serve with a meal.

NUTRITION INFORMATION PER SERVING:

Calories: 90 **Protein:** 4 g **Total carbohydrates:** 13 g
Fiber: 2 g **Total fat:** 3 g **Sodium:** 93 mg
Calcium: 90 mg **Omega-3 Fats (ALA):** 0 mg

Raita with Mushrooms

Simple – Serves 6

Crimini mushrooms provide minerals such as selenium, copper, potassium, phosphorus, manganese and zinc; vitamins such as B1, B2, B6, pantothenic acid and niacin and phytonutrients. The common button mushrooms, including crimini, have been shown to have anti-cancer properties.[8,9,10]

INGREDIENTS:

Olive oil (or **ghee** or **butter**)	1 T
Cumin seeds	½ t
Onion small, minced	1 (3 T)
Crimini mushrooms sliced	½ lb (2 Cups)
Yogurt low fat, dairy or non-dairy, plain	1 ½ Cups
Cumin ground	½ t
Salt	¼ t
Black pepper freshly ground	¼ t
Nutmeg	¼ t

DIRECTIONS:

1. Assemble and prepare all ingredients.

2. Heat a 1-quart pan with cumin seeds; when the seeds give off their aroma add oil and chopped onion; sauté.

3. When onion is tender add mushrooms; stir and cook covered on medium heat for 5 to 7 minutes. Allow cooling.

4. Combine yogurt, salt, black pepper, ground cumin and nutmeg. Mix well.

5. Add cooled mushroom mixture to the yogurt mixture. Stir well.

6. Serve with khichadi (p. 94), rice, bread, baked potato or any grain dish.

VARIATIONS & OPTIONS

- Substitute any other mushrooms for crimini mushrooms.

- Use a combination of garlic, onion and mushrooms for this raita.

- Substitute black mustard seeds for cumin seeds.

NUTRITION INFORMATION PER SERVING:

Calories: 67 **Protein:** 4 g **Total carbohydrates:** 6 g
Fiber: 0.5 g **Total fat:** 3 g **Sodium:** 96 mg
Calcium: 106 mg **Omega-3 Fats (ALA):** 20 mg

Raita with Potato

Simple – Serves 8

Cold potatoes provide the benefits of resistant starch (p. 67-68). A good quality yogurt contains live bacteria that promote gastro-intestinal health while supporting the immune system. Yogurt provides iodine, calcium, phosphorus, potassium, molybdenum and zinc; and vitamins B2, B12 and pantothenic acid as well as protein.[8,9]

INGREDIENTS:

Potatoes cooked diced . . . . .4 Cups

Yogurt low fat, dairy or non-dairy, plain . . . . 1½ Cups

Salt . . . . to taste or ¼ t

Cumin ground . . . . .1 t

Red chili pepper or **black pepper** . . . . to taste or ¼ t

Black mustard seeds coarsely ground . . . . ½ t

DIRECTIONS:

1. Assemble and prepare all ingredients.

2. Combine all the ingredients together; stir to mix well.

3. The raita can be prepared a day before you plan to serve which gives potatoes time to absorb the yogurt dressing. Add more yogurt if you need to.

VARIATIONS & OPTIONS

- Substitute plain greek yogurt for regular plain yogurt.

- Substitute cooked chickpeas for part or all of the potatoes.

- Add 2 T finely chopped onion, chives or scallions to the potato raita.

- Add chopped tomato or colored peppers and cilantro or parsley to the raita.

NUTRITION INFORMATION PER SERVING:
Calories: 98 **Protein:** 4 g **Total carbohydrates:** 19 g
Fiber: 1.5 g **Total fat:** 1 gram **Sodium:** 75 mg
Calcium: 85 mg **Omega-3 Fats (ALA):** 10 mg

Raita with Coconut and Cilantro

Simple – Serves 8

Cilantro (coriander) has been shown to lower blood sugar in animals. In parts of India it has traditionally been used as an anti-inflammatory agent. Cilantro's exceptional phytonutrient content, flavonoids and active phenolic acid compounds contribute to its healing properties. According to Ayurveda cilantro is cooling and aids digestion.[8,9]

INGREDIENTS:

Yogurt low fat, dairy or non-dairy, plain. . . . . .1 ½ Cups

Ginger fresh or frozen, grated. . . . . ½ t

Hot green chili pepper minced . . . . ½ t

Cumin ground . . . . .1 t

Salt . . . . to taste or ¼ t

Coconut unsweetened, finely grated . . . . ⅓ Cup

Cilantro chopped with tender stems . . . . 1 Cup

DIRECTIONS:

1. Assemble and prepare all ingredients.

2. Combine all ingredients together; mix well.

3. Serve raita with a meal, over a grain or with khichadi (p. 94).

4. For color and variety, add diced tomato or diced colored sweet pepper.

VARIATIONS & OPTIONS

- Add either grated cucumber or carrots to the raita.

- Add chopped tomatoes and scallions or Vidalia onion to the raita.

- Add cooked, cubed potato and/ or cooked beans to the raita for benefits of resistant starch (p. 67-68).

- Add fresh cut baby spinach to the raita.

NUTRITION INFORMATION PER SERVING:
Calories: 51 **Protein:** 3 g **Total carbohydrates:** 4 g
Fiber: 1 gram **Total fat:** 2.5 g **Sodium:** 73 mg
Calcium: 80 mg **Omega-3 Fats (ALA):** 0 mg

www.FeedingHealth.com

Raita with Eggplant

Elaborate – Serves 8

Turmeric has been used in Chinese and Indian medicine as an anti-inflammatory agent. Curcumin, the active ingredient in turmeric, has anti-inflammatory effects. Phytonutrients in eggplant include phenolic compounds and flavonoids, potent antioxidant and free radical scavengers, shown to protect cell membranes from damage. Eggplant provides minerals such as potassium, manganese, copper and magnesium and B vitamins.[8,9,10]

INGREDIENTS:

Eggplants medium, 6" by 4" (approximate size) . . . . 6 Cups (2)
Garlic unpeeled . . . . .4 cloves
Canola oil . . . . 1 T
Yogurt low fat, dairy or non-dairy, plain. . . . . .2 Cups
Salt . . . . to taste or ½ t
Turmeric . . . . .1 t
Cumin ground . . . . .1 t
Ginger fresh or frozen, grated. . . . . ½ t
Green chili pepper minced . . . . ½ t
or **red** or **black pepper** ground. . . . . ¼ t
Cilantro chopped with tender stems . . . . 1 Cup

DIRECTIONS:

1. Assemble and prepare all ingredients; preheat oven to 500°F.

2. Rub oil on the outside of eggplants and unpeeled garlic.

3. Turn oven down to 400°F; roast eggplants and garlic for 20 to 25 minutes. Check to be sure eggplant is fully cooked and soft in the center.

4. Take garlic out; leave eggplants in the oven while you work on other ingredients.

5. Peel and mash garlic with a fork; combine with yogurt, salt, turmeric, cumin, hot chili, ginger and cilantro.

6. Once eggplants are cool mash and add to yogurt mixture; mix well.

7. Serve raita with a meal.

8. Eggplants and garlic may also be roasted in foil on an outdoor grill in the summer.

VARIATIONS & OPTIONS

- Roast colored sweet peppers, zucchini and/or plum tomatoes with eggplant and garlic to make raita. Taste and adjust spices if volume of vegetables increases significantly.

- Substitute parsley, dill or basil for cilantro.

- Add ½ cup cooked chickpeas or lentils to raita for increasing resistant starch (p. 67-68).

NUTRITION INFORMATION PER SERVING:
Calories: 73 **Protein:** 4 g **Total carbohydrates:** 9 g
Fiber: 2 g **Total fat:** 3 g **Sodium:** 121 mg
Calcium: 113 mg **Omega-3 Fats (ALA):** 160 mg

Garlic in Yogurt

Simple – Serves 8

Garlic contains sulfur molecules, many of which are shown to function as antioxidants with anti-inflammatory properties. Garlic supplies the minerals manganese, phosphorus, selenium, calcium, potassium and copper; and vitamins B1, B6 and C.[8,9,10]

INGREDIENTS:

Yogurt dairy or non-dairy, plain, low fat. . . . . .2 Cups

Salt . . . . to taste or ⅛ t

Black or **red pepper** or **paprika** . . . . ¼ t

Oil (or **ghee**) . . . . .2 t

Cumin seeds. . . . . ½ t

Cloves whole 3

Asafetida (hing) . . . . pinch

Garlic sliced. . . . . .2 cloves

DIRECTIONS:

1. Assemble and prepare all ingredients.

2. Add salt and pepper to yogurt and mix well.

3. In small skillet heat oil with cumin seeds and cloves.

4. When cloves swell add asafetida and garlic; fry for 1-2 minutes; add this vaghar to the yogurt; stir to mix well.

5. Serve this yogurt with any meal but especially with khichadi (p. 94) or muthia (p. 113). It is also good as a dip for vegetables.

VARIATIONS & OPTIONS

- Add grated carrot or cucumber to this garlic yogurt.

- Add lightly steamed, chopped spinach to this yogurt and use as a dip for vegetables.

- Add leftover cooked potato, cubed small, to the yogurt.

- Add cooked or canned chickpeas or any other beans (for resistant starch (p. 67-68)) to yogurt.

NUTRITION INFORMATION PER SERVING:
Calories: 50 **Protein:** 3 g **Total carbohydrates:** 5 g
Fiber: 0 g **Total fat:** 2 g **Sodium:** 65 mg
Calcium: 103 mg **Omega-3 Fats (ALA):** 110 mg

Kadhi (Yogurt Chickpea Flour Soup)

Elaborate – Serves 6

- Add one or any combination of the following ingredients to the kadhi:

  - Chopped onion and garlic as part of the vaghar.

  - 2 cups sliced mushrooms as part of the vaghar.

  - Cooked mung beans or any other cooked bean can be added to the kadhi half way into the cooking process.

  - Cooked and cut potatoes, cooked cut okra, frozen peas or cut tomatoes may be added half way into the cooking process.

- Kadhi freezes well.

- Adjust the consistency of the kadhi by either increasing or decreasing the amount of water used or increasing or decreasing the amount of chickpea flour used.

INGREDIENTS:

Yogurt low fat, dairy or non-dairy, plain. . . . . .2 Cups
Chickpea flour . . . . ¼ Cup
Water . . . . .2 Cups
Salt . . . . ½ t
Ginger fresh or frozen, grated. . . . . .1 t
Fenugreek seeds . . . . ½ t
Jalapeño or **green chili pepper** minced. 1
Turmeric . . . . ¾ t
Oil (or ghee) . . . . 1 T
Cloves whole 6
Cinnamon stick. 1
Black mustard seeds . . . . ½ t
Cumin seeds. . . . . ½ t
Asafetida (hing) . . . . pinch
Curry leaves (limbdo, available in South Asian stores) optional
Mint fresh chopped. . . . . ¼ Cup
or **Cilantro** chopped . . . . ⅓ Cup

DIRECTIONS:

1. Assemble and prepare all ingredients.

2. Mix first 8 ingredients (ending with turmeric), using a beater to smooth out chickpea flour lumps.

3. Heat a heavy-bottomed 3-quart pot with cloves, cinnamon stick, mustard and cumin seeds. Before the seeds begin to pop add oil, asafetida, curry leaves and yogurt chickpea flour mixture.

4. Stir; bring to a boil, stirring frequently, on medium to medium- high heat. Kadhi will thicken slightly.

5. When it comes to a boil, turn heat off and add mint or cilantro.

6. Serve kadhi with any khichadi (p. 94) or with rice and beans.

NUTRITION INFORMATION PER SERVING:
Calories: 92 **Protein:** 5 g **Total carbohydrates:** 9 g
Fiber: 1 gram **Total fat:** 4 g **Sodium:** 163 mg
Calcium: 149 mg **Omega-3 Fats (ALA):** 230 mg

www.FeedingHealth.com

Nuts and seeds are very nourishing and make good snack foods. Nuts provide 8% to 18% of their calories in the form of protein. Although they are high in fat, this fat is all unsaturated, with the exception of coconut. Seeds provide 11% to 25% of their calories from protein. Most nuts are good sources of potassium, iron, magnesium, copper, selenium, and zinc, as well as E and B vitamins such as thiamin, niacin and riboflavin.[8,9,10] Almonds, Brazil nuts, filberts (hazelnuts) and sesame seeds contain more calcium than other nuts and seeds. Sunflower, pumpkin, squash and sesame seeds contain iron, potassium and phosphorus. Seeds provide even more fiber than nuts. Flax seeds are a good source of omega-3 fats.[8,9]

Condiments

Dry Sesame Chutney Spice Mixture

Simple – Serves 20

Sesame seeds provide the minerals copper, manganese, magnesium, calcium, iron, phosphorus and zinc, along with vitamin B1, fiber and monounsaturated fats. In a study in the Journal of Agricultural and Food Chemistry, researchers published the amounts of phytosterols present in nuts and seeds commonly eaten in the United States. Sesame seeds had the highest total phytosterol content (400-413 mg per 100 grams). Phytosterols are naturally occurring compounds within plants. Ingesting phytosterols, in foods, may help you control your cholesterol levels, aid in joint health and in boosting your immune system. Good sources of phytosterols include rice bran, corn, wheat germ, flax seed, nuts and legumes, oranges, bananas, beetroot and Brussels sprouts.[8,9,10]

INGREDIENTS:

Sesame seeds	2 Cups
Salt	to taste or ½ t
Cumin seeds	2 t
Garlic sliced	3 cloves
Hot red chili peppers dry, whole	2 to 3
Cilantro chopped with tender stems	3 T

DIRECTIONS:

1. Assemble and prepare all ingredients.

2. In a preheated heavy-bottomed skillet toast – separately – sesame seeds, cumin seeds, sliced garlic and whole dry red peppers; allow cooling.

3. In the warm skillet, with heat off, lightly toast chopped cilantro; be sure it does not burn.

4. Add salt to taste to the cooled roasted ingredients and grind, pulsing only till sesame seeds are still coarse.

5. Store in a tightly sealed glass container and refrigerate or freeze for longer storage.

6. Use over baked or boiled potatoes, top any vegetable, plain yogurt, bean or grain.

7. Serve with Puda, savory pancakes (p. 109).

VARIATIONS & OPTIONS

- Substitute peanuts, walnuts or any other nuts or seeds for sesame seeds.

- Add 2 T flax seeds for part of the sesame seeds to increase omega-3 fat content. Do not toast the flax seeds.

- Add more garlic if you like.

- Add more or less of the whole dry hot red chili peppers according to taste.

- You can reduce salt, eliminate it or use a salt substitute if you prefer.

NUTRITION INFORMATION PER SERVING:
Calories: 88 **Protein:** 4 g **Total carbohydrates:** 2 g
Fiber: 1 gram **Total fat:** 8 g **Sodium:** 35 mg
Calcium: 21 mg **Omega-3 Fats (ALA):** 0 mg

Sesame Tahini Sauce

Simple – Serves 4

Using lemon or lime for flavoring provides several benefits. I use lemon and lime juice freely for taste, nutrition and to replace some of the salt in a recipe. Citrus fruits provide vitamin C, increase the absorption of calcium and iron, are alkaline in the body and add some sour taste to food. Lemons in particular contain monoterpenoids, such as d-limonene, which assist the body in detoxifying itself.[5,6,9]

INGREDIENTS:

Tahini	¼ Cup
Garlic crushed	1 clove
Salt	⅛ t
Lemon or **lime** juiced	1

DIRECTIONS:

1. Assemble and prepare all ingredients.

2. Mix all ingredients together, beating with a fork.

3. Enjoy this sauce on asparagus, baked potato, sandwich spread, with artichokes or use your creativity and enjoy with other foods.

NUTRITION INFORMATION PER SERVING:
Calories: 89 **Protein:** 3 g **Total carbohydrates:** 5 g
Fiber: 1 gram **Total fat:** 7 g **Sodium:** 46 mg
Calcium: 65 mg **Omega-3 Fats (ALA):** 0 mg

Dill, Sesame Tahini and Orange Juice Dressing

Simple – Serves 4

Dill leaves are rich in beta-carotene, iron and potassium. Dill seed is a good source of calcium, manganese and iron as well as important phytonutrients. Black pepper improves digestion and promotes intestinal health.[8,9,10]

INGREDIENTS:

Garlic fresh small cloves. 2

Dill leaves fresh, with tender stems, lightly packed. . . . . . .2 Cups

Sesame tahini. . . . . 1 ½ T

Salt . . . . ¼ t

Black pepper freshly ground . . . . ¼ t

Orange juice concentrate. . . . . 2 T

Water . . . . ⅓ Cup

DIRECTIONS:

1. Assemble and prepare all ingredients.

2. In a blender first chop garlic; then add dill and blend.

3. Next blend in tahini, salt and pepper.

4. Blend in orange juice concentrate and water.

VARIATIONS & OPTIONS

- Substitute ½ cup orange juice in place of concentrate and water.

- Adjust garlic according to taste.

- Substitute cilantro, basil, mint or parsley for dill.

- To use this as a dip or spread add more tahini or less liquid to change consistency.

NUTRITION INFORMATION PER SERVING
Calories: 43 **Protein:** 1 gram **Total carbohydrates:** 4 g
Fiber: 1 gram **Total fat:** 3 g **Sodium:** 78 mg
Calcium: 37 mg **Omega-3 Fats (ALA):** 0 mg

www.FeedingHealth.com

Basic Cilantro Green Chutney

Simple – Similar to Pesto

Cilantro (coriander) has a variety of phytonutrients in addition to being a very good source of fiber, iron, magnesium and manganese. Many of its healing properties are due to its exceptional phytonutrient content.[8,9]

INGREDIENTS:

Cilantro with tender stems . . . . ½ pound
Long hot peppers . . . . to taste or ¼ pound, 3
Ginger fresh. . . . . .1" piece
Peanuts. . . . . ½ Cup
Water . . . . ½ Cup
Cumin ground . . . . .1 t
Salt . . . . to taste or ½ t
Lemon or **lime** juiced 1

DIRECTIONS:

1. Assemble and prepare all ingredients.

2. In a food processor or powerful blender, grind cilantro, hot peppers, ginger and peanuts. Add water to help with blending.

3. Add ground cumin, salt and lemon juice. Blend to a smooth puree.

4. Use it as you would use pesto. Stir it into steamed vegetables, mashed potatoes, cooked grains and beans or soups to enhance the flavors. Use it as a spread on a sandwich, such as a cheese and chutney sandwich with tomato and cucumber slices.

5. Add this chutney to baked or grilled tofu or tempeh cubes.

6. Freeze extra chutney in ice cube trays, then pack the frozen cubes in a zip lock bag or container for use another time.

Carrot Pickle
Simple

Mustard seeds and powder, like other Brassicas, contains plenty of phytonutrients. Isothiocyanates in mustard seed and other Brassicas have been repeatedly studied for their anti-cancer effects.[8,9] *Carrots contain vitamins A (as beta-carotene), C and K, and the mineral potassium. Beta-carotene's powerful antioxidant actions help provide protection against macular degeneration and the development of senile cataracts which are the leading cause of blindness in the elderly.*[8,9,10]

INGREDIENTS:

Carrots sliced diagonally or grated . . . . .3 Cups
Lemon or **lime** juiced. 1
Oil . . . . 1 T
Mustard seeds coarsely ground . . . . .½ tsp
Salt. . . . . .¼ tsp
Hot green chilies or **jalapeno peppers** thin sliced 1-2
*The chili peppers are only for flavor – you won't be eating
    them unless you choose to.*

DIRECTIONS:

1. Assemble and prepare all ingredients.
2. Combine lemon juice, oil, salt and ground mustard seeds; whisk with a fork.
3. Add sliced green chilies and carrots; mix well.
4. Cover and allow to marinate for a day or two in the refrigerator.
5. Enjoy as a condiment with a meal or on a sandwich.

VARIATIONS & OPTIONS:

- Add blanched cut cauliflower or shredded cabbage to carrots; adjust seasoning if needed.

- Use a combination of sliced and blanched root vegetables such as turnips, parsnips with carrots, cabbage and cauliflower.

Understanding Fiber

Fiber, a carbohydrate, is an important nutrient that, while not contributing any calories, has health-promoting benefits. Fiber is the indigestible part of plant cells available in all plant foods. For a long time it was believed that there were two kinds of fiber: soluble and insoluble. Nutrition research over the last 20 years has uncovered a third kind: resistant starch. All three are essential, and each has specific health benefits. Sugars and most starches are digested in the small intestine, where they are rapidly absorbed and used for short-term energy needs or stored. Resistant starch and dietary fiber are not digested in the small intestine, instead passing through to the large intestine, where they are either fermented or are eliminated from the body unaltered.

Recently, the Institute of Medicine has categorized fiber into:

Dietary fiber, which consists of non-digestible carbohydrates and lignin present in whole unprocessed plant foods, and

Functional fiber, which consists of isolated non-digestible carbohydrates (not found in whole foods) that have been added to processed foods (E.g. some breakfast cereals).

 Soluble fiber feeds the intestinal bacteria, which produce short chain fatty acids that produce a number of positive effects in the body by nourishing the cells of the large intestine. Soluble fiber, found in oatmeal, barley, rye, beans, peas and lentils, fresh and dried fruits, and most vegetables, helps lower blood cholesterol and control blood sugar.

Insoluble fiber helps digestion by trapping water in the colon and by inactivating intestinal toxins. It provides bulk and helps keep us "regular." Good sources are whole grains and legumes, skins and seeds of fruits and vegetables.

Resistant starch is any starch or starch product that is not digested in the small intestine. Traditionally, it was assumed that all starch was broken into sugars and absorbed in the small intestine. However, resistant starch, as the name implies, resists digestion in the small intestine and passes to the large bowel. Here, intestinal bacteria ferment resistant starch. The products of this fermentation process, short chain fatty acids, improve colon health and have been shown to prevent the growth and proliferation of colorectal cancer cells in rats. Resistant starch has the properties of both soluble and insoluble fiber – it provides stool bulk and keeps you "regular" and is fermented to provide a healthy environment for "good" gut bacteria. Resistant starch is naturally found in under-ripe bananas (those which have green ends), legumes, whole grains, *and in cooked-then-cooled starchy foods such as rice, potatoes or pasta, tapioca and some corn varieties.*

Because resistant starch is not digested and absorbed as sugars in the small intestine, it causes lower blood sugar levels than other, digestible starches. Lower blood sugars are also associated with lower blood insulin levels in many people. Lower blood sugar and insulin levels are desirable in people with diabetes as they help prevent complications such as kidney failure and loss of feeling in the extremities (neuropathy). It can also be beneficial for healthy people, as blood sugar and insulin levels that spike repeatedly can contribute, at least in part, to metabolic abnormalities. One of these abnormalities, insulin resistance, is associated with the development of obesity, diabetes, dyslipidemia (high triglycerides – high "bad" cholesterol), hypertension (high blood pressure) and cardiovascular disease.

Recently, it has been shown that eating resistant starch can increase the amount of fat you burn after a meal. However, this effect is unlikely to cause weight loss, because the total amount of calories burned after eating resistant starch is exactly the same as if you ate a regular, digestible starch. So, resistant starch changes the type of fuel you burn rather than the amount of fuel that you burn. Even though this effect won't lead to weight loss, it may be beneficial for maintaining muscle mass and preventing fat accumulation during weight maintenance.

BENEFITS OF RESISTANT STARCH:
1. Helps maintain a healthy colon and digestive system.
2. Lowers the blood sugar and insulin impact of foods that you eat.
3. Increases fat burning after a meal.
4. Increases uptake of important minerals, such as calcium.
5. As a pre-biotic fiber, selectively stimulates the growth and activity of beneficial bacteria in the colon, especially bifid bacteria and Lactobacillus.

SUMMARY
A well-balanced diet containing a variety of fruits, vegetables, legumes and whole grains contains a mixture of different types of dietary fiber, each of which contributes to health. Fiber in foods such as beans, whole grains, vegetables, and *cooked-then-cooled starchy foods* will delay blood sugar from rising quickly after eating and thus help stabilize blood sugar while keeping your diet low in fat. Intake of both soluble and insoluble fiber has been shown to be beneficial in reducing the risk of diabetes and cardiovascular disease. Because fiber-rich meals are low in calorie density, they prolong feelings of satiety and may reduce hunger and subsequent food intake.

Janine Higgins, PhD
Nutrition Research Director
Clinical Translational Research Center (CTRC)
University of Colorado, Denver

Gita Patel MS RD CDE LD

Archaeological evidence shows legumes are among the oldest agricultural crops, dating back some 10,000 years. Legumes have been found in Egyptian tombs and are frequently referred to in the Bible. Beans and legumes come in a stunning variety of shapes, sizes and colors. They are readily available, inexpensive and easy to prepare. Main dishes around the world rely on beans, which are powerhouses of nutrients – from France's cassoulets and Brazil's black bean soups to the Middle East's hummus, Spain's boiled beef and chickpeas, Mexico's refritos, Native America's succotash, New England's baked beans, Nigeria's black-eyed pea fritters, China's crunchy bean sprouts, Japan's sweet adzuki bean paste and India's wide variety of daals and bean dishes.[8]

In Ayurveda, beans are used for cleansing and nourishing health. Split mung beans, used in preparing daal and khichadi (p. 94), a popular staple in India, are highly regarded in Ayurveda, as they are lighter and easier to digest than most other beans.[12]

What we eat is the most important building block of health and beans offer many health benefits, including phytonutrient saponins, antioxidant anthocyanins, protein, complex carbohydrates, fiber and resistant starch (p. 67-68). The darker the bean, the more antioxidant anthocyanins it contains. Beans also contain an abundant quantity of the antioxidant inositol hexaphosphate. Phytonutrients enhance the body's natural defenses against chronic diseases. Fiber supports healthy estrogen metabolism, digestive health and increases satiety.[8,9]

Beans & Legumes

Antioxidants inhibit the reactions of free radicals. Free radicals cause damage to the DNA, cells and tissues, resulting in inflammation. Antioxidants from nutrients in our diets are first-line defenders, suppressing oxygen free radicals and other reactive oxygen and nitrogen species that contribute to chronic diseases. They even repair damage caused by those radicals.[1,2]

Most phytonutrients have antioxidant properties that help our bodies fight harmful chronic inflammation, thus reducing our risk of associated diseases, including cancer, atherosclerosis, macular degeneration and diabetes. Phytonutrients disrupt established pro-inflammatory pathways.[1,2,3]

Beans and legumes provide minerals including zinc, magnesium, phosphorous, potassium, calcium, copper, manganese and iron and B vitamins – thiamin, riboflavin, niacin and folic acid[8,9]

The Glycemic Index (GI) ranks carbohydrate foods (sugars and starches) on a scale from 0 to 100 according to the extent and the rapidity with which they raise blood sugar levels after being eaten. Beans and legumes have a low glycemic index and a low glycemic load per serving, are cholesterol free, and contain protein ranging from 22% to 25% with soy providing even more protein.[13]

Plants produce phytonutrients for their own self-defense, as protection against viruses, fungi and bacteria. Phytonutrients are concentrated in the bran and the germ – hence the importance of eating beans and whole grains.[8,9]

All of these nutrients and benefits come without trans-fat, cholesterol or sodium, and may help reduce the risk of heart disease, type 2 diabetes and various cancers. They lower blood cholesterol and help reduce blood pressure. Beans are digested slowly, thus resulting in a gradual rise in blood sugar – a great benefit, especially for people with diabetes.

TIPS:

1. Before cooking or sprouting dry beans and legumes, it is important to search through them to remove any tiny sticks or small stones. Rinse the beans in several changes of water, cover with water by at least two inches and then let them soak overnight or for 7 to 24 hours. Dry beans can be cooked without soaking but soaking helps soften and reconstitute the beans, reduces cooking time as well as fuel costs and enhances the beans' digestibility. Beans will re-hydrate to 2 to 3 times their dry size. Drain off the soaking water and rinse beans again before cooking. Cover beans by at least one inch of fresh water; add a teaspoon of oil to reduce foaming and boil-over; bring beans to a boil; reduce heat to low, cover and simmer beans gently for about an hour or until cooked al dente. Avoid over-cooking. Increase soaking and cooking times in hard water or high altitude areas.

2. Acidic ingredients such as lemon juice, lime juice, vinegar or tomatoes prevent beans from tenderizing so add these ingredients after beans are fully cooked and tender.

3. Consider these quick, easy ways to add beans to your diet: Use them to top salads, add to your favorite salsa or pesto, soup or stew; cook with grains or make into spreads, pâtés and dips. Sprout them, too – sprouting beans increases their nutrients and digestibility, removing lectins and reducing cooking times. Use beans as side dishes or as main dishes for breakfast, lunch or dinner.

4. If you are not accustomed to using beans in your diet making khichadi (p. 94) is a good way to start. Khichadi combines a grain and a bean and is easy to digest.

5. Initially, consider using the smaller beans – mung beans, adzuki beans, green or black lentils. These require less cooking time and are easier to digest.

Chickpeas

Simple – Serves 8

Chickpeas (garbanzo beans) contain the minerals molybdenum, manganese, copper, phosphorus and iron; as well as folate, protein and fiber. Both the outer layer and the large main inner portion of garbanzo beans contain antioxidant and anti-inflammatory nutrients.[8,9]

INGREDIENTS:

Chickpeas cooked (or canned) . . . . .4 Cups
Turmeric . . . . .1 t
Canola oil . . . . 1 T
Water, for cooking . . . . .2 ½ Cups
Cumin ground . . . . .1 t
Salt . . . . ¼ t
Lemon or **limejuice** . . . . .to taste or 1
Cilantro chopped with tender stems . . . . ½ Cup
Red or **black pepper** or **fresh green chili pepper** minced
. . . . .to taste, ¼ to ½ t

DIRECTIONS:

1. Assemble and prepare all ingredients.
2. Rinse soaked (soak 8-24 hours) chickpeas before cooking. Cook covered with turmeric, oil and water till tender but al dente.
3. To the cooked (or canned) beans add cumin, salt, lime or lemon juice, cilantro and pepper. Stir to mix the ingredients well.
4. Enjoy as a side dish, in a pita pocket, as a snack by itself or with a meal.

VARIATIONS & OPTIONS:

- Cook extra chickpeas for the freezer; use some to make any of the recipes that follow.

- Substitute cooked black, cannellini or mung beans for chickpeas.

- Add cooked chickpeas to raita (p. 49), salsa or pasta sauce or make hummus. The chickpeas in the raita and hummus provide the benefits of resistant starch (p. 67-68).

- Make chickpea salad by adding any one or more of the following: Chopped tomato, diced cucumber, diced onion, chopped chives or scallion, corn, shredded cabbage, baby spinach, diced avocado and/or diced under ripe mango.

- Substitute parsley or any other herb for cilantro.

NUTRITION INFORMATION PER SERVING:
Calories: 150 **Protein:** 7 g **Total Carbohydrates:** 23 g
Fiber: 6.5 g **Total fat:** 4 g **Sodium:** 41 mg
Calcium: 42 mg **Omega-3 Fats (ALA):** 200 mg

Chickpeas in Chickpea Flour Sauce

Elaborate – Serves 6

INGREDIENTS:

Chickpeas cooked (or canned) . . . . .4 Cups
Cumin seeds. . . . . ¼ t
Black mustard seeds . . . . ¼ t
Cinnamon . . . . 1 stick
Cloves whole 6
Hot pepper dried, whole (optional). 1
Canola oil . . . . 2 T
Asafetida (hing) . . . . pinch
Garlic chopped . . . . .2 cloves
Chickpea flour . . . . 2 T
Water . . . . 1 Cup
Salt . . . . ¼ t
Coriander-cumin powder (p. 132). . . . . 1 T
Dates chopped. . . . . 2 T
Cayenne pepper. . . . . ⅛ t
Lemon juiced . . . . to taste
Cilantro chopped with tender stems . . . . ½ Cup

DIRECTIONS:

1. Assemble and prepare all ingredients.

2. Heat a large heavy-bottomed pan on medium-high heat with cumin and mustard seeds, cinnamon stick, cloves and whole dry red pepper.

3. Before the seeds pop, reduce heat to low, add oil, asafetida and garlic; stir and turn heat off; add chickpea flour stirring to prevent the flour from burning.

4. Add water and the rest of the ingredients; turn heat to medium high; bring to a boil; turn heat off.

5. Serve with a grain and salad or vegetable.

6. This can also be used as a topping on a baked potato.

7. Substitute tamarind paste for lemon or lime.

VARIATIONS & OPTIONS:

- Substitute small red adzuki beans for chickpeas.

- Substitute kidney beans for chickpeas.

- Substitute finely chopped onion for garlic or use both together.

- Substitute another dried fruit for the dates.

- Substitute another flour for chickpea flour.

NUTRITION INFORMATION PER SERVING:

Calories: 185 **Protein:** 8 g **Total Carbohydrates:** 26 g
Fiber: 7 g **Total fat:** 6 g **Sodium:** 45 mg
Calcium: 53 mg **Omega-3 Fats (ALA):** 370 mg

Chickpeas in Tomato Sauce

Simple – Serves 8

VARIATIONS & OPTIONS:

- Substitute coarsely ground almonds, cashews, pistachios or walnuts for coconut.

- Substitute any other bean, pea or legume for chickpeas.

- Substitute 4 cups of cubed potatoes or cauliflower for chickpeas.

- Substitute a combination of cauliflower, potato, carrot and peas for chickpeas.

- Add baby spinach or any other dark green leafy vegetable with chickpeas in step 4 of the recipe.

- Freeze leftovers for another meal.

Substitute garam masala (p. 133) (2 T or to taste) for the cinnamon, cardamom and coriander-cumin powder in this recipe, if you have it handy with your spices. Herbs and spices, in use since approximately 5,000 B.C.E., are among the richest sources of antioxidants.

INGREDIENTS:

Chickpeas cooked (or canned) . . . . .4 Cups
Canola oil . . . . 1 t plus 2 T
Onions medium, minced 2
Red peppers dried, whole 2
Tomatoes diced (tomato puree or tomato juice, 3 Cups) 3
Ginger fresh or frozen, grated. . . . . .1 ½ t
Garlic minced . . . . .3 cloves
Coriander-cumin powder (p. 132). . . . . 2 T
Turmeric. . . . . .1 t
Salt . . . . to taste or ½ t
Cinnamon ground . . . . ½ t
Cardamom ground . . . . ½ t
Coconut dried, unsweetened, grated. . . . . 2 T
Cilantro chopped with tender stems . . . . 1 Cup
Lemon or **limejuice**. . . . . to taste

DIRECTIONS:

1. Assemble and prepare all ingredients.

2. Heat a 3-quart pan with oil, minced onions and whole dry red pepper; fry till onions are light brown and translucent.

3. Add tomatoes, ginger and garlic; stir and reduce heat to medium.

4. Add coriander-cumin powder, turmeric, salt, cinnamon powder, ground cardamom, cooked chickpeas and coconut.

5. Cook covered for 7 to 10 minutes stirring frequently.

6. Add cilantro and lime or lemon juice before serving with a grain and salad or vegetable.

NUTRITION INFORMATION PER SERVING:
Calories: 215 **Protein:** 9 g **Total Carbohydrates:** 31 g
Fiber: 8.5 g **Total fat:** 7 g **Sodium:** 86 mg
Calcium: 74 mg **Omega-3 Fats (ALA):** 410 mg

Chickpeas Roasted with Turmeric

Simple Snack – Serves 4

In traditional Chinese and Ayurvedic medicine, turmeric has been used to support digestion and liver function, relieve arthritis pain and to regulate menstruation. Turmeric, rich in potassium and iron, contains a chemical called curcumin, which has antioxidant, anti-cancer and anti-inflammatory properties. Its pungent, bitter and slightly astringent properties stimulate those taste buds.[8,9,12]

INGREDIENTS:

Chickpeas cooked al dente (or canned) . . . . .2 Cups
Turmeric . . . . ½ t
Canola oil . . . . .1 t
Cumin ground . . . . ½ t
Coriander ground . . . . 1½ t
Salt . . . . to taste or ⅛ t
Black or **red chili pepper** ground. ½ t
Lemon or **lime juice** . . . . 1 T

DIRECTIONS:

1. Assemble and prepare all ingredients.
2. Mix all of the ingredients together; let them sit for 1 to 3 hours.
3. When ready to roast preheat oven to 500°F.
4. Spread the mixed ingredients on a rimmed baking sheet.
5. Turn heat down to 375°F and roast them for 30 minutes or until chickpeas are crisp on the outside and slightly tender on the inside.
6. Enjoy a tasty, low fat and phytonutrient rich snack.
7. Refrigerate or freeze leftovers.

VARIATIONS & OPTIONS:

- Substitute cooked adzuki beans, lentils or mung beans for chickpeas. Cook smaller beans al dente. They will take less baking time, so check them in 20 minutes.

- If in a hurry, use any canned beans instead of cooking dry beans. Rinse and towel dry canned beans before adding other ingredients.

- Add ½ t garlic powder to the mixture.

- For a sweet snack, mix adzuki beans cooked al dente, with ¼ cup maple syrup, ½ t oil and 1 to 2 T cocoa powder. Stir well; set aside for 1 to 2 hours; then roast in the oven as per the recipe. The smaller beans may roast in a shorter time and lower temperature (350°F) than the chickpeas.

NUTRITION INFORMATION PER SERVING:
Calories: 151 **Protein:** 7 g **Total Carbohydrates:** 24 g
Fiber: 7 g **Total fat:** 3.5 g **Sodium:** 42 mg
Calcium: 49 mg **Omega-3 Fats (ALA):** 150 mg

Mung Bean Sprouts Salad

Simple – Serves 4

During sprouting, trypsin inhibitors in beans and legumes that impair digestibility are inactivated. During germination, lentils synthesize B-vitamins and vitamin C in a form that is easy to digest and absorb.[8,9] To make your own sprouts (p. 144) at home, use 1 cup dry mung beans or lentils to produce 4 to 4 ½ cups sprouts, depending on their length. Store-bought lentil sprouts may also be used. If using store-bought Chinese bean sprouts, do not add water with the beans.

INGREDIENTS:

Canola oil	1 T
Cumin seeds	¼ t
Black mustard seeds	¼ t
Asafetida (hing)	pinch
Garlic sliced	2 cloves
Mung bean sprouts homegrown, packed	4 Cups
Water	¼ Cup
Turmeric	½ t
Salt	to taste or ¼ t
Lemon zest	¼ t
Cayenne	to taste or ⅛ t
Lemon juice	to taste
Cilantro chopped with tender stems	½ Cup

DIRECTIONS:

1. Assemble and prepare all ingredients.
2. Combine sprouts, water, turmeric, salt, lemon zest and cayenne; set aside.
3. Heat a 2-quart skillet on high with cumin and mustard seeds.
4. Before the seeds pop add oil, asafetida and garlic; reduce heat to medium-high.
5. Immediately add sprouts mixture. Stir to mix well.
6. Cover and cook 5 minutes on medium-high or till desired, stirring 1-2 times.
7. Add lemon juice to taste, stir to mix and garnish with chopped cilantro.
8. Serve with a grain, as a side dish or use as a filling in a wrap or pita pocket. I enjoy them alone for lunch.
9. Cooked mung bean sprouts (home grown) can be frozen; cook extra for the freezer.

VARIATIONS & OPTIONS:
- Use these Ingredients:

Oil	2 T
Black mustard seeds	⅓ t
Asafetida	pinch
Garlic chopped	2 cloves
Jalapeño sliced in half	1
Mung bean sprouts	4 cups
Carrots grated	3 cups
Water	¼ cup
Turmeric	½ t
Salt	to taste or ¼ t
Lime juiced	one-half
Cilantro chopped with tender stems	1 cup
Sesame seeds or coconut, dried, unsweetened, grated	2 T

Cook the same as in the recipe and garnish with chopped cilantro and coconut.

- In the summer, I cook mung bean sprouts with fresh corn kernels following the original recipe. It tastes very good and also freezes well.

- Consider stir-frying shredded cabbage or sliced colored sweet peppers with sprouts in the recipe.

- I enjoy a combination of cauliflower, fresh corn and sprouts cooked together.

- Add sprouts and garam masala (p. 133) to a rice dish to make a pulav.

NUTRITION INFORMATION PER SERVING:
Calories: 70 **Protein:** 3 g **Total Carbohydrates:** 8 g
Fiber: 2 g **Total fat:** 4 g **Sodium:** 78 mg
Calcium: 22 mg **Omega-3 Fats (ALA):** 350 mg

Dry Green Pea Ragdo (Dry Green Pea Curry)

Elaborate – Serves 8

From my sister Madhu

INGREDIENTS:

Green peas dry	2 Cups
Water for cooking green peas	3 Cups
Turmeric	¾ t
Black mustard seeds	1 t
Coconut unsweetened dry	½ Cup
Garam masala (p. 133)	1 t
Green chilies hot, slit in half	2
Canola oil	2 T
Onions medium, finely chopped	2
Garlic minced	6 cloves
Ginger grated fresh or frozen	2 t
Tomatoes medium, finely chopped	2
Salt	½ t
Cilantro (reserve some for garnish) chopped with tender stems	½ Cup
Lemon or lime juiced	1

DIRECTIONS:

1. Assemble and prepare all ingredients.

2. Cook soaked (7-24 hours), drained and rinsed dry green peas in 3 cups water and turmeric.

3. Lightly dry roast in a small skillet on medium heat, black mustard seeds. Turn heat off when they begin to change color but leave on the heated burner.

4. Add coconut, garam masala and slit green chilies to the hot mustard seeds in the skillet and stir. Leave in the hot skillet on the burner.

5. In a heavy bottomed 3-quart pan sauté chopped onions in oil till translucent.

6. Add garlic, ginger and chopped tomatoes; sauté for 3 – 4 minutes.

7. Add cooked peas with their water and salt; stir to mix and add roasted ingredients in the small skillet and continue cooking on medium heat for 8-10 minutes.

8. Add cilantro and lemon juice before serving. Serve with a meal or baked potato.

NUTRITION INFORMATION PER SERVING:
Calories: 193 **Protein:** 8 g **Total Carbohydrates:** 24 g
Fiber: 8 g **Total fat:** 8 g **Sodium:** 164 mg
Calcium: 20 mg **Omega-3 Fats (ALA):** 310 mg

Gujarati Mung Beans Daal

Elaborate – Serves 6

In Gujarat, our daals (daar in Gujarati) always have a sweet and sour taste. In fact, Gujarati cuisine is known for its sweet and sour foods. Unprocessed raw brown sugar – jaggary (gaur) or dates – traditionally sweetens Gujarati foods. Traditionally, many Gujaratis were farmers who did physical work on farms. However, our lifestyles are different and in the interest of reducing calories, I have omitted the sugar.

VARIATIONS & OPTIONS:

- Substitute green or black french lentils, kidney beans or dry peas for mung beans.

- To sweeten the daal add ½ cup chopped dates in step 5 of the recipe.

- Substitute ½ cup diced under ripe mango pieces for the lemon or limejuice.

- Substitute black pepper for the cayenne pepper.

- Substitute 1 to 2 T of tomato paste or ½ cup tomato purée for fresh tomato.

- The cayenne pepper is optional. The other spices add flavor and nutrients without the heat. If you eliminate the cayenne this makes a nice soup.

- If you use ½ to 1 cup less water to cook the beans then you have a drier dish with less sauce. This then makes a nice spread on a cracker for a snack, as an appetizer or to fill a pita pocket, wrap or sandwich.

- If it is spicier than you like (added too much cayenne?), adjust the heat by adding yogurt and eating it with a plain grain or even topping a baked potato.

- This recipe freezes well, so be sure to cook extra for the freezer.

INGREDIENTS:

Mung beans dry	1 Cup
Water	3 Cups
Turmeric	¾ t
Cumin seeds	¼ t
Black mustard seeds	¼ t
Cinnamon stick	2"
Cloves whole	6
Canola oil (or ghee)	2 T
Asafetida	pinch
Onion red, medium, sliced	1
Garlic crushed	2 cloves
Ginger fresh or frozen, grated	1 t
Tomato diced	1 chopped
Salt	½ t
Coriander-cumin powder (3:1) (p. 132)	1 T
Cayenne pepper ground	¼ t
Coconut dried, unsweetened, grated	1 T
Cilantro chopped with tender stems	½ Cup
Lemon or **lime**, juiced	to taste

DIRECTIONS:

1. Assemble and prepare all ingredients.
2. Cook the soaked, rinsed and drained mung beans in 3 cups water and turmeric.
3. Heat a 2-quart pot with cumin and mustard seeds, cinnamon stick and cloves.
4. Before the seeds begin to pop add oil, asafetida and onion; sauté till onion is translucent.
5. Add garlic, ginger and tomato; stir to mix; add cooked mung beans with the cooking water, salt, coriander-cumin powder, cayenne pepper and coconut; simmer for 5 to 10 minutes on medium heat.
6. Before serving add lemon or limejuice and garnish with cilantro.
7. Serve with basmati rice, millet or quinoa along with yogurt and vegetables or salad.

NUTRITION INFORMATION PER SERVING:
Calories: 189 **Protein:** 9 g **Total Carbohydrates:** 27 g
Fiber: 7 g **Total fat:** 6 g **Sodium:** 105 mg
Calcium: 68 mg **Omega-3 Fats (ALA):** 450 mg

Gujarati Tuver Daal (Split Pigeon Peas Daal)

Simple – Serves 6

INGREDIENTS:

Split pigeon peas dry (tuver daal)	1 Cup
Water	2 Cups
Peanuts	⅓ Cup
Dates chopped	⅓ Cup
Tomatoes fresh, diced	2
Salt	½ t
Turmeric	1 t
Cayenne pepper (or **Jalapeño** sliced, 1)	¼ t
Ginger fresh or frozen, grated	1 ½ t
Coriander-cumin powder (p. 132)	2 T
Canola oil	2 T
Red pepper dry, whole	1 (optional)
Cinnamon stick	1
Cloves whole	6
Fenugreek seeds	1 t
Black mustard seeds	½ t
Asafetida	pinch
Lemon or **lime** juiced	2 T
Cilantro chopped with tender stems	½ Cup

DIRECTIONS:

1. Assemble and prepare all ingredients.

2. Cook rinsed, soaked and rinsed pigeon peas in 2 cups water.

3. Combine 2 cups water, peanuts, dates, tomatoes, salt, turmeric, cayenne or Jalapeño, ginger and coriander-cumin powder; set aside.

4. Heat a 2-quart pan with cinnamon stick, cloves, fenugreek and mustard seeds and whole red dry pepper.

5. Before the seeds start popping, add oil, asafetida and the water mixture.

6. Add cooked and mashed/puréed pigeon peas. Bring to a boil; simmer 5 minutes.

7. Before serving add cilantro and lemon or limejuice.

8. Daal (daar) is served as part of a meal with rice, roti (p. 103), and a vegetable.

VARIATIONS & OPTIONS:

- Add ¼ cup split channa daal to the 1 cup pigeon peas; cook them together.

- Cook 2 cups diced carrots with the tuver daal.

- Add 1 - 2 T garam masala (p. 133) to the daal with cilantro and lemon or limejuice.

- Substitute tomato juice, tomato paste or tomato purée for fresh tomatoes.

- Substitute yellow split peas for the split pigeon peas.

- Substitute fresh or dry coconut for the peanuts.

- In the fall I have also added a few cranberries in step 5 with the water mixture.

- Substitute ½ cup diced under ripe mango for the lemon or limejuice.

- Cook eggplant, zucchini or squash with the pigeon peas.

NUTRITION INFORMATION PER SERVING:
Calories: 168 **Protein:** 5 g **Total Carbohydrates:** 17 g
Fiber: 5 g **Total fat:** 10 g **Sodium:** 126 mg
Calcium: 44 mg **Omega-3 Fats (ALA):** 450 mg

Sundal

Simple – Serves 6

This recipe is from my niece Darshana, who lives in South India. Chili peppers contain a substance called capsaicin. The hotter the chili pepper, the more capsaicin it contains. Red chili peppers are shown to reduce blood cholesterol, triglyceride levels, and platelet aggregation.[8,9,14]

INGREDIENTS:

Yellow peas (soak 12-24 hours), whole dry . . . . 1 Cup
Water for cooking. . . . . .1 ⅓ Cups
Turmeric . . . . ½ t
Salt . . . . ¼ t
Black mustard seeds . . . . ¼ t
Canola oil . . . . 1 T
Asafetida (hing) . . . . pinch
Hot chili pepper whole, dry 1
Curry leaves (neem if available) . . . . 5 to 6
Hot green chili minced 1
Coconut dry, grated, unsweetened . . . . 2 T
Cilantro chopped with tender stems . . . . ½ Cup
Mango raw or under ripe, diced small . . . . ½ Cup
If mango is unavailable, use apple, lime or lemon juice

DIRECTIONS:

1. Assemble and prepare all ingredients.
2. Cook the soaked and rinsed peas al dente with turmeric and water.
3. Heat a 2-quart pan with mustard seeds. Before the seeds begin to pop, add oil, asafetida, whole red chili pepper and curry leaves (if available).
4. Add cooked yellow peas, salt and minced green chili; stir to mix and cook on low heat for 5 – 7 minutes.
5. Garnish with grated coconut, cilantro and the diced mango.
6. Serve as an appetizer, snack or as part of a meal.

VARIATIONS & OPTIONS:

- Substitute black-eyed peas, red kidney beans, green mung beans, lentil or chickpeas for the yellow peas. They all taste good.

NUTRITION INFORMATION PER SERVING:
Calories: 150 **Protein:** 8 g **Total Carbohydrates:** 19 g
Fiber: 8 g **Total fat:** 4 g **Sodium:** 197 mg
Calcium: 18 mg **Omega-3 Fats (ALA):** 140 mg

Pinto Beans

Simple – Serves 4

Pinto beans provide the minerals molybdenum, manganese, phosphorus, iron, magnesium, potassium and copper, as well as vitamin B1, folate and protein. Certain phytonutrients in pinto beans are shown to be helpful in preventing some cancers, including stomach cancer. A cup of cooked pinto beans provides 58.8% of the recommended daily intake for fiber.[8,9,10]

INGREDIENTS:

Canola oil	4 t
Cumin seeds whole	½ t
Onion red, medium, chopped	1
Garlic chopped	2 cloves
Tomato paste mixed with ¼ Cup water	2 T
Turmeric	½ t
Cilantro chopped with tender stems	½ Cup
Cayenne pepper	⅛ t
Salt	to taste
Pinto beans cooked al dente (or canned)	2 Cups

DIRECTIONS:

1. Assemble and prepare all ingredients.
2. Heat cumin seeds in a heavy bottomed 1-quart pan on medium high heat.
3. When seeds give off an aroma add oil, chopped onion and garlic; sauté 2-3 minutes.
4. Add tomato paste with water or tomato purée, turmeric, cilantro, cayenne and salt to taste. Mix well; reduce heat to medium.
5. Add cooked beans, stir well and cook 5 - 7 minutes.
6. Serve with rice or any other grain such as millet, barley, quinoa or amaranth.
7. Freeze leftovers for another meal.

VARIATIONS & OPTIONS:

- Substitute black pepper for cayenne pepper.
- Substitute parsley for cilantro.
- Add fresh or frozen grated ginger to this recipe.
- Substitute any other bean for pinto beans.
- In season use fresh tomatoes in place of tomato paste or tomato purée.
- Use either onion or garlic.

NUTRITION INFORMATION PER SERVING:
Calories: 185 **Protein:** 9 g **Total Carbohydrates:** 28 g
Fiber: 9 g **Total fat:** 9 g **Sodium:** 78 mg
Calcium: 55 mg **Omega-3 Fats (ALA):** 540 mg

Lentil Salad with Avocado & Mango

Elaborate – Serves 8

Lentils provide the minerals molybdenum, manganese, iron, phosphorus, copper and potassium; vitamin B1 and folate; as well as fiber and protein, with virtually no fat. A whole cup of cooked lentils has only 230 calories.[8,9,10] *The lentil salad also provides the benefits of resistant starch (p. 67-68).*

INGREDIENTS:

French lentils cooked al dente in 2½ Cups water . . . . 1½ Cups
Sweet red peppers roasted (or unroasted) and cut in strips 2
Avocado ripe, cubed 1
Mango under ripe, cut in small pieces 1
Red onion small, minced . . . . ½ Cup
Cilantro chopped with tender stems . . . . 1 Cup
Salt . . . . ½ t
Cayenne black pepper or chili pepper . . . . ½ t
Cumin ground . . . . 1 t
Lemon juice and zest 1

DIRECTIONS:

1. Assemble and prepare all ingredients.

2. Cut sweet peppers in half, remove seeds and veins; roast peppers with inside facing down in a preheated oven at 500°F, under the broiler for approximately 3 minutes.

3. Put roasted peppers in a covered bowl for 5 to 7 minutes to steam. Scrape off the charred skins and cut peppers into squares or strips.

4. Combine cooked lentils, red peppers, cubed avocado, mango, onion, cilantro, salt, cayenne, ground cumin, lemon zest and lemon juice.

5. Enjoy the salad with a meal or by itself on a bed of romaine lettuce or mixed greens.

VARIATIONS & OPTIONS:

- Substitute chickpeas, black beans, black-eyed beans or kidney beans for lentils.

- Add 1 cup of roasted corn kernels to the salad.

- Add 1 clove of minced garlic.

- Add 2 T chopped mint.

- Substitute parsley, marjoram or thyme for cilantro.

- Substitute oranges or pineapple for mango and orange zest in place of lemon zest.

NUTRITION INFORMATION PER SERVING:
Calories: 181 **Protein:** 9 g **Total Carbohydrates:** 30 g
Fiber: 8 g **Total fat:** 4 g **Sodium:** 79 mg
Calcium: 29 mg **Omega-3 Fats (ALA):** 50 mg

Corn and Bean Salad

Simple – Serves 8

Among fruits, avocados are the richest source of lutein, alpha and gamma tocopherols, beta-carotene and small amounts of zeaxanthin and cryptoxanthin, along with other carotenoids, phytosterols, chlorophyll, polyphenols and glutathione. The carotenoids are concentrated just beneath the peel. Carotenoids are fat-soluble, so the fat in the avocado helps in their absorption. Lutein, the major antioxidant in avocados, accumulates in the macular region of the human retina. Macular degeneration is the most common cause of blindness in Americans over 65. Avocados contain a variety of phytonutrients, fiber and vitamins such as B6, C, K and folate plus minerals such as copper and potassium.[8,9,10] This salad also provides the benefits of resistant starch (p. 67-68).

INGREDIENTS:

Corn kernels fresh or frozen . . . . .3 Cups
Olive oil. . . . . .1 t
Salad beans canned, drained, 15-ounce can 1
Salt. . . . . ¼ t
Cumin ground . . . . .1 t
Jalapeño finely chopped. . . . . one-half
Red onion finely minced . . . . ½ Cup
Avocado cut into small pieces. 1
Mango under ripe, cut into small pieces. 1
Cilantro chopped with tender stems . . . . 1 Cup
Lemon juiced. 1

DIRECTIONS:

1. Assemble and prepare all ingredients.
2. Preheat the oven to 500°F.
3. Add 1 t olive oil to the corn, mix well and spread on a rimmed cookie sheet.
4. Reduce oven temperature to 450°F and roast corn for 10 minutes. Turn oven off and leave corn inside until needed.
5. Combine drained salad beans, salt, cumin, jalapeño, onion, avocado, mango, cilantro, lemon juice and roasted corn. Mix well.
6. Serve on a bed of mixed greens, romaine lettuce, baby spinach, watercress or arugula, or enjoy alone as a salad for lunch or part of a meal.

VARIATIONS & OPTIONS:

- Substitute cooked or canned chickpeas, black beans, white cannellini beans or green lentils for canned salad beans.

- Substitute any other fruit, such as kiwi, apple, pineapple, peach or pear for mango.

- Substitute freshly ground black or red chili pepper for jalapeño.

- Cook beans with a little turmeric for extra antioxidants.

- Add diced tomatoes, cucumbers and grated carrot to the salad.

NUTRITION INFORMATION PER SERVING:
Calories: 156 **Protein:** 5 g **Total Carbohydrates:** 28 g
Fiber: 6 g **Total fat:** 4.5 g **Sodium:** 101 mg
Calcium: 30 mg **Omega-3 Fats (ALA):** 50 mg

Sweet and Sour Adzuki Beans

Elaborate – Serves 6

Beans contain an abundant quantity of inositol hexaphosphate, an antioxidant. The darker the beans the more anthocyanins they contain.[8,9]

INGREDIENTS:

Adzuki beans dry	1 Cup
Water	1½ Cups
Black mustard seeds	¼ t
Cumin	¼ t
Cinnamon	1 stick
Cloves whole	5
Canola oil	1 T
Asafetida (hing)	pinch
Garlic crushed	½ t
Chickpea flour (besan)	1-heaped T
Water	½ to 1 Cup
Ginger fresh or frozen, grated	½ t
Coriander-cumin powder (p. 132)	1 T
Turmeric	¼ t
Cayenne pepper ground	⅛ t
Dates chopped	5
Salt	¼ t
Lemon or **lime** juiced	2 T
Cilantro chopped with tender stems for garnish	½ Cup

DIRECTIONS:

1. Assemble and prepare all ingredients.
2. Cook soaked and rinsed beans al dente in 1½ cups water.
3. Combine ½ cup water, ginger, coriander-cumin powder, turmeric, salt, cayenne and chopped dates; set aside.
4. In a heavy-bottomed 2-quart pan heat cumin and mustard seeds, cinnamon stick and cloves.
5. Before the seeds pop, add oil, asafetida, garlic and chickpea flour.
6. Reduce heat; stir to mix and add water mixture; bring to a boil.
7. Stir and add cooked beans; cook covered on low for 5-7 minutes.
8. Before serving add lemon or limejuice and cilantro.
9. Serve with rice or grain and a vegetable.
10. Freeze leftovers for another meal.

NUTRITION INFORMATION PER SERVING:
Calories: 142 **Protein:** 7 g **Total Carbohydrates:** 24 g
Fiber: 8 g **Total fat:** 3 g **Sodium:** 49 mg
Calcium: 54 mg **Omega-3 Fats (ALA):** 140 mg

Kidney Beans
Simple – Serves 4

Kidney beans contain the minerals molybdenum, manganese, phosphorus, iron, copper, magnesium and potassium; vitamins B1, K and folate as well as fiber and protein.[8,9,10]

INGREDIENTS:

Cumin seeds	½ t
Canola oil	1 T
Onion large, minced	1
Garlic minced	3 cloves
Ginger fresh or frozen, grated	1 t
Cinnamon ground	¼ t
Cloves ground	⅛ t
Turmeric	½ t
Cayenne pepper ground	¼ t
Salt	¼ t
Cilantro chopped with tender stems	½ Cup
Kidney beans home-cooked (or canned)	2 Cups

DIRECTIONS:

1. Assemble and prepare all ingredients.
2. In a 2-quart pan, heat cumin seeds.
3. When the seeds give off an aroma add oil and chopped onion; sauté for a few minutes.
4. Add garlic, ginger, cinnamon, cloves, turmeric, cayenne, salt and cilantro.
5. Stir to mix well and add kidney beans.
6. Mix well and cook covered till all ingredients are blended and heated through.
7. Serve with a grain and vegetable.

VARIATIONS & OPTIONS:

- Substitute any other cooked bean for kidney beans.
- Substitute green or black lentils for kidney beans.
- Use a combination of beans and spinach or any other dark green leafy vegetable.
- Top a baked potato with these beans.

NUTRITION INFORMATION PER SERVING:
Calories: 162 **Protein:** 9 g **Total Carbohydrates:** 25 g
Fiber: 9 g **Total fat:** 3.5 g **Sodium:** 77 mg
Calcium: 77 mg **Omega-3 Fats (ALA):** 30 mg

Whole grains contain hundreds of phytonutrients such as phytoestrogens, antioxidants, phenols, soluble and insoluble fiber, resistant starch (p. 67-68) and complex carbohydrates, in addition to significant amounts of B vitamins (riboflavin, thiamin, and niacin), vitamin E, iron, zinc, calcium, selenium and magnesium. They are very low in fat and have protein content averaging 10% – 12%.[8,9]

Grains are considered high in carbohydrates. However, not all carbohydrate foods produce the same blood sugar response. The type of carbohydrate food you eat is important. Ask yourself: is it processed? Does it contain lots of white sugar and fat but no fiber? Is the carbohydrate whole and in its natural form? The brain, red blood cells, retinal cells, and liver and kidney cells all need carbohydrate (glucose) for energy. The difference in carbohydrates between potato chips, mashed potatoes, cold potato salad and a whole baked potato can be explained by the glycemic index.

The glycemic index (GI) ranks carbohydrate containing foods on a scale from 0 to 100 according to the extent and the rapidity with which the blood sugar levels rise after the foods are eaten.

Whole, unprocessed plant foods that contain intact fiber move more slowly through the gastrointestinal tract than those whose fiber has been removed. This provides a feeling of fullness, which helps prevent overeating. The recipes in this book are all healthful, providing fiber and phytonutrients essential for feeding health.

Research suggests that eating more low GI foods such as those found in the recipes in this book may result in:

1. Reduced risk for heart disease
2. Prevention of type 2 diabetes
3. Reduced risk for complications in individuals with diabetes
4. Decrease in appetite
5. Increased energy levels

The GI of a food is affected by many different factors. Here are some things to consider:

1. Cooking can cause some carbohydrates to swell and burst, making their starch more easily digested and more quickly converted to blood sugar – which results in a higher GI score. Therefore, it is important not to overcook grains, but to serve them al dente, cooked but firm: they should still offer some resistance "to the tooth."
2. Food processing can also destroy the outer coating of some carbohydrates, making them easier to digest and resulting in a higher GI score.
3. Fiber and resistant starch in a food slow the digestion and absorption of carbohydrates, resulting in a lower GI score.
4. Fat also slows the digestion and absorption of carbohydrates, which results in a lower GI score. Healthful fats such as olive oil, nuts, seeds and avocado can be used creatively to lower the GI of a food.
5. Protein-containing foods such as legumes (high in fiber and resistant starch p. 67-68), vegetables like edamame (green soybeans) and nuts have a low GI score.
6. Combining other foods with carbohydrate-rich foods influences your glycemic response to them. Make sure your meal or snack is "complex" and contains unprocessed complex carbohydrates (e.g., whole grains and whole fresh fruits), protein, healthy fats and fiber to keep blood glucose levels within the normal range.

TIPS
1. Store whole grains in tightly closed containers in a dry place. If you freeze grains, they will keep almost indefinitely. The exceptions are oats and oat bran, which are higher in fat than other grains. Because of this they can turn rancid.
2. Before cooking any grain, scan through it to remove any unwanted natural materials such as stones or sticks. Rinse the rice or grain and then soak it in a measured amount of water for up to 7-8 hours for faster cooking. Soaking the larger whole grains reduces cooking time. The smaller grains such as amaranth, millet or quinoa do not require soaking. If you do not have time to soak, you can still follow these recipes, but cooking time may be longer.

Basmati Rice Brown or White

Simple – Serves 4

Rice contains the trace mineral manganese as well as selenium and magnesium.[8] It is an important part of Indian cuisine and is eaten daily by people around the world.

INGREDIENTS:

Basmati rice brown or white. . . . . 1 Cup
Water . . . . 1½ Cup
Salt. . . . . ¼ t

DIRECTIONS:

1. Assemble and prepare all ingredients.

2. Bring rice, salt and water to a boil; reduce heat, cover and simmer till tender. Cook al dente. Note that brown rice will take 2-3 times as long to cook as white rice.

3. You can cook rice covered on the stove top, in a rice cooker or covered in the oven, at 350°F for 30 to 40 minutes, checking once or twice to see whether rice is cooked al dente.

4. Serve with daal or beans and vegetables.

5. Leftover rice can be frozen or refrigerated. Thaw frozen rice slowly in the refrigerator.

6. The section on fiber discusses resistant starch (p. 67-68) in cooked and cooled grains. So, enjoy leftover rice as a cold rice salad; eat it separately with a vegetable, a green salad or soup to get the benefits of resistant starch.

VARIATIONS & OPTIONS:

- Add ½ t turmeric to any variation that follows except when saffron is added.

- Add one or more of the following: 4-6 cloves, 1 cinnamon stick, ½ t turmeric, 3 whole cardamom pods cracked open and/or a bay leaf to make the rice very aromatic.

- Add 1 to 2 cups green peas, diced carrots or mixed vegetables to rice during cooking.

- Try a vaghar of 2 T oil, butter or ghee with ¼ t of cumin seeds. When the seeds are roasted add rice, water, salt and turmeric; cook till al dente.

- Use a vaghar of oil, butter or ghee with 1 stick cinnamon and 6 whole cloves; optional is the addition of ⅓ cup nuts (cashews, slivered almonds, or pistachios); add rice, turmeric and water; cook al dente.

- Season oil or ghee with cinnamon stick, 2 whole cardamom pods (cracked open); add rice, water, salt, a pinch of saffron, 1 cup peas, ¼ cup nuts and ¼ cup raisins. Cook.

- Substitute millet, quinoa or any other grain for basmati rice in all the variations.

- Season oil or ghee with cinnamon stick, 4 cloves, ¼ t cumin seeds and 1 small thinly sliced onion. Sauté onion for 2 minutes; then add rice, water, salt, turmeric, ¼ t grated ginger and 1 cup cut vegetables. Cook covered till tender.

NUTRITION INFORMATION PER SERVING:
Calories: 160 **Protein:** 4 g **Total carbohydrates:** 34 g
Fiber: 2 g **Total fat:** 2 g **Sodium:** 70 mg
Calcium: 0 mg **Omega-3 Fats (ALA):** 0 mg

Rice with Cabbage and Peas

Elaborate – Serves 8

INGREDIENTS:

Cinnamon	2 3" sticks
Cloves whole	6
Canola oil	2 T
Onion large, sliced	1
Cardamom green, whole pods broken open.	3
Cabbage (red or green), finely shredded	3 Cups
Basmati rice brown	1-½ Cups
Water	2 ½ Cups
Salt	¼ t
Cashews or **almonds**, slivered	¼ Cup
Garam masala (p. 133)	1 t
Cayenne pepper ground	¼ t
Turmeric	1 t
Jalapeño pepper chopped.	½ t
Ginger fresh or frozen, grated.	1 t
Garlic chopped	3 cloves
Green peas	1 Cup
Lemon or **lime**, juiced	2 T
Cilantro chopped with tender stems	1 Cup

DIRECTIONS:

1. Assemble and prepare all ingredients.
2. Combine rice, water, salt, nuts, garam masala, cayenne, turmeric, jalapeño, garlic and ginger; set aside.
3. Heat a heavy-bottomed 3-quart pan on medium-high heat with cinnamon sticks, cloves, oil and sliced onion; sauté for 2 to 3 minutes.
4. Add cardamom and cabbage; stir and cook for 2-3 minutes.
5. Add rice and water mixture; stir and bring to a boil; reduce heat, cover and simmer for 10 minutes.
6. Add peas, cilantro and lemon juice. Stir, cover and cook till rice is al dente.
7. Serve with kadhi (p. 59), raita (p. 49) or plain yogurt and stir-fried mung bean sprouts or any other vegetable.

VARIATIONS & OPTIONS:

- Add more garam masala according to taste.
- Add 1 cup chopped red peppers or grape tomatoes in step 6 for color and taste.
- Substitute edamame for green peas to increase protein and make it a one-dish meal.
- Substitute millet, quinoa or barley for basmati rice. Millet and quinoa take less cooking time than barley.
- Add mung beans, lentil or soy sprouts in place of peas.

NUTRITION INFORMATION PER SERVING:

Calories: 206 **Protein:** 5.5 g **Total carbohydrates:** 34 g
Fiber: 4 g **Total fat:** 5.5 g **Sodium:** 42 mg
Calcium: 35 mg **Omega-3 Fats (ALA):** 340 mg

Barley and Baby Crimini Mushrooms

Elaborate – Serves 6

Barley provides fiber as well as the minerals selenium, phosphorus, copper and manganese. Mushrooms are a good source of vegetable protein, providing over 35% of calories from protein. They are low in calories and contain B vitamins and minerals such as copper. Some varieties contain antibacterial, anti-tumor and other medicinal substances.[8,9,10] Barley contains gluten, so individuals with gluten sensitivity (p.146) can substitute another grain.

INGREDIENTS:

Barley	1 Cup
Water	2 Cups
Black mustard seeds	1 t
Cloves whole	3
Canola oil	2 T
Asafetida	pinch
Onion chopped	1
Baby crimini mushrooms sliced	10 ounces
Sesame seeds	2 T
Salt	½ t
Turmeric	1 t
Black pepper	¼ t
Parsley chopped	1 Cup

DIRECTIONS:

1. Assemble and prepare all ingredients.
2. Cook soaked barley al dente.
3. Combine onion, mushrooms and sesame seeds; set aside.
4. Heat a 2-quart pan with mustard seeds and cloves; when the seeds change color add oil, asafetida and combined vegetables.
5. Stir; add salt and turmeric. Cook covered for 4 to 5 minutes.
6. Add the almost-cooked barley, parsley and black pepper; stir to mix well and cook till mushrooms and barley are tender.
7. Serve with a green salad or vegetable and kadhi (p. 59), raita (p. 49) or plain yogurt.

VARIATIONS & OPTIONS:
- Substitute millet, rice or quinoa for barley.
- Substitute cilantro for parsley.
- Add 1 cup grated carrots, diced red peppers or halved grape tomatoes in step 6.

NUTRITION INFORMATION PER SERVING:
Calories: 202 **Protein:** 6 g **Total carbohydrates:** 32 g
Fiber: 7 g **Total fat:** 6.5 g **Sodium:** 106 mg
Calcium: 70 mg **Omega-3 Fats (ALA):** 480 mg

Amaranth

Simple – Yields 2 cups cooked, Serves 4

Amaranth is the only grain with significant vitamin C and calcium. One-half cup dry amaranth seeds contain as much calcium as 3 cups of raw broccoli, 1 ounce of blue cheese or ½ cup of cow's milk. It is also a good source of magnesium, potassium, folic acid and iron. Amaranth has more protein than most other grains, providing 16% protein by weight.[8,9]

INGREDIENTS:

Amaranth	1 Cup
Salt (optional)	⅛ t
Turmeric	¼ t
Cinnamon	1 3" stick
Water	1½ Cup

DIRECTIONS:

1. Assemble and prepare all ingredients.

2. Add amaranth, salt, cinnamon stick and turmeric to the water. Cook on high to bring to a boil. Reduce heat and simmer covered for 15 to 20 minutes till tender.

3. Serve as a side dish with a vegetable or salad, kadhi (p. 59), raita (p. 49), beans or daal.

VARIATIONS & OPTIONS:

- Serve amaranth for breakfast; cook it in a mixture of fruit juice and water. Or stir in 1 to 2 T frozen concentrated fruit juice (apple, grape, pineapple or orange), and serve it with yogurt, fresh fruit and a few nuts. Or serve it with yogurt or milk, fresh fruit, a few nuts, and cinnamon, cardamom or a dash of nutmeg.

- For lunch use cooked amaranth to make a tabouli or other cold salad.

- Serve as a grain with dinner.

- Do a vaghar with 1 T of oil and ¼ t of cumin or black mustard seeds; add a small chopped onion and sauté. Then add 1 cup amaranth, water, salt and ⅛ t turmeric. Cook till tender. When almost cooked stir in ½ cup frozen green peas.

NUTRITION INFORMATION PER SERVING:
Calories: 183 **Protein:** 7 g **Total carbohydrates:** 32 g
Fiber: 4.5 g **Total fat:** 3 g **Sodium:** 10 mg
Calcium: 75 mg **Omega-3 Fats (ALA):** 0 mg

Quinoa

Simple – Yields 2 cups cooked, Serves 4

Quinoa is a relative of leafy green vegetables like spinach and Swiss chard. It was once considered "the gold of the Incas." Quinoa has a nutty flavor, low glycemic index and provides 16% protein by weight with over 10 g in a 1 cup serving, along with nutrients such as manganese, calcium, iron, magnesium, copper, phosphorus and B vitamins.[8,9] Quinoa seeds are naturally coated with a film of resin called "saponin," and they need to be rinsed several times in warm water before cooking to remove this resin.[8]

INGREDIENTS:

Quinoa gold, red, or black . . . . 1 Cup
Water . . . . 1½ Cups
Salt (optional) . . . . ⅛ t
Turmeric . . . . ¼ t
Cinnamon . . . . 1 3" stick

DIRECTIONS:

1. Assemble and prepare all ingredients.

2. Add water, salt, turmeric and cinnamon stick to the rinsed quinoa and bring to a boil; reduce heat, cover and simmer till tender, for 12 to 15 minutes.

3. Serve as a side dish with a vegetable or salad, kadhi (p. 59), raita (p. 49) or beans.

VARIATIONS & OPTIONS:

- Use quinoa to make a pasta or tabouli type of cold salad.

- Substitute millet for quinoa.

- For breakfast, cook rinsed quinoa in fruit juice or half-diluted fruit juice. Serve with yogurt and fresh fruit. Or serve cooked quinoa with fresh fruit, nuts and yogurt or milk.

- For a rich nutty flavor, lightly toast the quinoa seeds (unwashed) without oil in a pan or skillet, stirring constantly, before adding water to cook the quinoa.

- Season 1 T of oil with ¼ t of cumin or black mustard seeds; add a small chopped onion, sauté; add green peas (or cut colored peppers), cooked quinoa, salt to taste, and ⅛ t turmeric. Cook for a few minutes till well mixed and garnish with herbs such as parsley or cilantro and chopped tomato.

- Leftover cooked (or uncooked) quinoa can also be added to soups.

NUTRITION INFORMATION PER SERVING:
Calories: 159 **Protein:** 6 g **Total carbohydrates:** 29 g
Fiber: 2.5 g **Total fat:** 2.5 g **Sodium:** 9 mg
Calcium: 26 mg **Omega-3 Fats (ALA):** 0 mg

Quinoa with Edamame

Elaborate – Serves 6

Onions contain vitamins B6, C and folate; as well as the minerals chromium, manganese, molybdenum, potassium, phosphorus and copper. They are low in calories and have high polyphenol content and a large amount of quercetin. Onion's antioxidants, such as quercetin, provide anti-inflammatory benefits. Onions may help reduce cholesterol levels, blood pressure and blood sugar.[8,9]

INGREDIENTS:

Cumin seeds	¼ t
Canola oil	1 T
Jalapeño chopped	one-third
Red onion minced	1 Cup
Quinoa	1 Cup
Water	1½ Cups
Edamame fresh or thawed frozen	1 Cup
Salt	⅛ t
Turmeric	¼ t
Cilantro chopped with tender stems	½ Cup
Orange juice frozen concentrated	3 T

DIRECTIONS:

1. Assemble and prepare all ingredients.

2. Heat cumin seeds in a 2-quart pan on medium-high heat till seeds give off an aroma.

3. Add oil, jalapeño and onion; sauté for a few minutes till onion is tender.

4. Add quinoa with water; bring to a boil; reduce heat and simmer covered for 5 minutes.

5. Add thawed edamame, salt and turmeric; stir and cook al dente.

6. Turn heat off and stir in orange juice concentrate and cilantro.

7. Serve with a vegetable or salad, kadhi (p. 59), raita (p. 49) or plain yogurt.

VARIATIONS & OPTIONS:

- Substitute black mustard seeds for cumin seeds.

- Substitute any other cooked bean for edamame.

- Substitute dried fruit for the orange juice concentrate.

- Substitute another herb for cilantro.

- Add garlic and ginger with the onion.

NUTRITION INFORMATION PER SERVING:
Calories: 181 **Protein:** 7 g **Total carbohydrates:** 27 g
Fiber: 3 g **Total fat:** 5 g **Sodium:** 34 mg
Calcium: 52 mg **Omega-3 Fats (ALA):** 220 mg

Beans & Grains

Khichadi

Simple – Serves 8

Khichadi is one of my family's favorite foods. The simplest everyday version is basmati rice and split mung beans or tuver daal (daar) cooked together with a little ghee or butter.

INGREDIENTS:

Mung beans split (mung daal)	¾ Cup
Water for beans	¾ Cup
Cinnamon	1" stick
Cloves whole	6
Turmeric	½ t
Salt	to taste or ½ t
Basmati rice	1½ Cups
Water for rice	2 ¾ Cups

DIRECTIONS:

1. Assemble and prepare all ingredients.

2. If using brown basmati rice wash and soak split mung beans and rice separately since brown rice takes longer to cook than split mung beans. If using white basmati rice, soak and cook rice and beans together.

3. Combine brown rice, water, cinnamon stick, cloves, turmeric and salt; bring to a boil; reduce heat, cover and cook 5 minutes.

4. Add split mung beans with water, stir and cook covered till tender – al dente.

5. Khichadi is served with kadhi (p. 59), raita (p. 49) or plain yogurt, plus a vegetable and a salad of chopped onion and tomatoes. Potatoes, okra, spinach or green beans go well with khichadi and kadhi.

6. Leftover khichadi can be frozen or refrigerated. Enjoy cold leftover khichadi with a green salad, vegetable or yogurt.

Note: Cold khichadi provides benefits of resistant starch (p. 67-68) so enjoy leftovers.

VARIATIONS & OPTIONS:

- Khichadi can take on endless variations depending on the combinations of split or whole beans, grains, herbs, spices and vegetables used in its preparation. Khichadi is easier to digest than most whole beans eaten alone. This makes a great complete one-dish meal. The following vaghar options are just some examples of the possibilities for this recipe: Prepare any one of the following vaghar (p. 13, 137) in ghee or oil:

- black mustard seeds and asafetida

- fenugreek seeds and asafetida

- whole black peppercorns

- cinnamon, cloves and cardamom

- cardamom and bay leaves

- ¾ t black mustard seeds, 1 cinnamon stick and 6 cloves: before the seeds begin to pop add 1 T oil or ghee, brown rice, water, turmeric and salt; cover and cook for 5 minutes. Add soaked split mung beans, stir and cook till al dente.

- ¾ t cumin and/or black mustard seeds, 1 stick cinnamon and 6 cloves; before the seeds begin to pop add 1 T oil or ghee and 1 thinly sliced onion; sauté 2 minutes. Add brown rice, water, turmeric, ½ t grated ginger and salt; cover and cook for 5 minutes. Add 1 cut hot pepper if desired. Add the soaked split mung beans, stir and cook al dente.

- Fennel seeds may be added to the plain khichadi.

- Garlic, ginger, chopped jalapeño, sliced or chopped onion and any vegetable may be added to the khichadi to make a one-dish, one-pot meal.

- Substitute whole mung beans, split pigeon peas, green or black lentils, chickpeas, adzuki beans or sprouts for split mung beans.

- Substitute millet, amaranth, quinoa, steel cut oats or barley for basmati rice to make khichadi. Allow your intuition and creativity to guide you. Try 1 cup pearl barley with ½ cup split mung beans khichadi.

NUTRITION INFORMATION PER SERVING:
Calories: 166 **Protein:** 6 g **Total carbohydrates:** 34 g
Fiber: 4 g **Total fat:** 1 gram **Sodium:** 72 mg
Calcium: 15 mg **Omega-3 Fats (ALA):** 0 mg

Asparagus Khichadi

Elaborate – Serves 8

VARIATIONS & OPTIONS:

- Substitute any other vegetable for asparagus.

- Substitute any other bean or legume such as edamame for split mung beans.

- Substitute sprouts (mung, lentil or soy) for split mung beans.

- Substitute another grain such as millet or quinoa for rice.

- Add an herb, such as dill, parsley or cilantro.

- Cooled leftovers provide benefits of resistant starch (p. 67-68) so enjoy this unheated for lunch.

Fenugreek seeds may also be sprouted and cooked with beans. Fenugreek leaves are eaten as a fresh green vegetable in India and added to daal, chapatti and other vegetables. Fenugreek improves insulin sensitivity in individuals with type 1 and type 2 diabetes and has been used to treat diabetes, constipation, and hyperlipidemia. Asparagus, a member of the lily family, provides over 50% of its calories from protein in addition to providing flavonoids, antioxidants, vitamins K, C, A, B1, B2, B3, B6 and folate; and minerals such as manganese, copper, phosphorus and potassium. Asparagus helps maintain a more alkaline environment in the body.[8,9,10]

INGREDIENTS:

Cumin seeds	½ t
Fenugreek seeds	½ t
Canola oil (or ghee)	2 T
Asafetida	pinch
Neem leaves (optional, available in Indian groceries)	4-6
Onion sliced	1
Split mung beans rinse, soak	¾ Cup
Basmati rice rinse, soak	1 ½ Cups
Water for beans and rice	3 ½ Cups
Salt	½ t
Turmeric	¾ t
or **saffron**	⅛ t
Cumin ground	½ t
Asparagus tips cut 4", rest cut 2"	1 lb (¾ lb trimmed)

DIRECTIONS:

1. Assemble and prepare all ingredients.

2. Heat a 3-quart pan with cumin and fenugreek seeds; before the seeds begin to pop, add oil or ghee, asafetida, neem leaves and sliced onion; sauté for 1-2 minutes.

3. Add soaked beans and rice with their soaking water, salt and saffron or turmeric.

4. Stir, cover and cook 10 -12 minutes, until rice grains are almost tender.

5. Add ground cumin and cut asparagus; stir to mix; cook until asparagus is crisp tender. (Or steam asparagus separately and stir into the finished khichadi.)

6. Serve with raita (p. 49), plain yogurt or kadhi (p. 59) and a salad or vegetable.

NUTRITION INFORMATION PER SERVING:
Calories: 207 **Protein:** 7 g **Total carbohydrates:** 38 g
Fiber: 5 g **Total fat:** 5 g **Sodium:** 74 mg
Calcium: 33 mg **Omega-3 Fats (ALA):** 310 mg

Barley and Mung Beans Khichadi

Elaborate – Serves 8

Barley is an excellent substitute for rice and other grains. It is high in both soluble and insoluble fiber and if you eat the leftover khichadi cold, you also get the benefit of resistant starch (p. 67-68). This offers additional health benefits beyond cholesterol reduction. Soluble fiber and resistant starch help maintain blood sugar levels, which may be beneficial in preventing and managing type 2 diabetes.[8,9] Barley contains gluten, so individuals with gluten sensitivity (p.146) can substitute another grain.

INGREDIENTS:

Canola oil (or ghee)	2 T
Cinnamon stick	1
Cloves whole	6
Onion chopped	1
Garlic sliced	2 cloves
Ginger fresh or frozen, grated	1 t
Jalapeño or other hot green pepper (optional) cut in half	1
Barley soaked overnight	1 Cup
Water for barley	1½ Cups
Salt	to taste or ½ t
Turmeric	1 t
Green mung beans whole, soaked overnight	1 Cup
Water for mung beans	1½ Cups

DIRECTIONS:

1. Assemble and prepare all ingredients.
2. If you have not soaked barley and mung beans overnight, rinse them separately, bring each to a boil in its own pan, cover, turn heat off and keep them on the stove for 1 to 2 hours before cooking. This reduces the cooking time.
3. Combine onion, garlic, ginger and jalapeno; set aside.
4. Heat oil or ghee in a 3-quart pan with the cinnamon stick, cloves and other combined ingredients; sauté for a few minutes.
5. Add barley with its water, salt and turmeric. Stir, cover and cook for 5 minutes before adding mung beans with their water.
6. Stir, cover and cook until water is absorbed – 15 to 20 minutes if the grains have been soaked for 12 - 24 hours. Cook al dente.
7. Serve with a vegetable or salad, plus kadhi, raita or plain yogurt.
8. This freezes well, so plan for the freezer, as well as enjoying the benefits of resistant starch by eating unheated leftovers the next day for lunch.

NUTRITION INFORMATION PER SERVING:

Calories: 217 **Protein:** 9 g **Total carbohydrates:** 37 g
Fiber: 8 g **Total fat:** 4 g **Sodium:** 77 mg
Calcium: 46 mg **Omega-3 Fats (ALA):** 350 mg

VARIATIONS & OPTIONS:

- To reduce cooking time, sprout barley and mung beans; then make khichadi.

- Make a simple khichadi with just cinnamon, cumin seeds, cloves and garam masala (p. 133) omitting the onion, garlic, ginger and/or jalapeño.

- I have added 1 t cumin seeds in step 4 and 1 pound of cut kale in step 5 with mung beans, to make a one-dish meal. Enjoy with a raita (p. 49), plain yogurt or kadhi (p. 59).

- Add 1 t black mustard seeds in step 4 and 2 T sesame seeds in step 5 of this recipe.

Lentil Sprouts and Rice Khichadi

Elaborate – Serves 8

Cinnamon has a long history both as a spice and as a medicine. Cinnamon is one of the oldest spices known. It is mentioned in the Bible and was used in ancient Egypt not only as a beverage flavoring and medicine, but also as an embalming agent.

VARIATIONS & OPTIONS:

- Substitute soy, mung beans or any other sprouts for lentils.

- Substitute any other grain such as quinoa, barley, millet or amaranth for rice.

- Substitute almonds, pistachios, pecans or walnuts for cashews.

- Substitute diced dates, dried apricots or dried peaches for raisins.

- Plan some for the freezer as well as enjoy benefits of resistant starch (p. 67-68) by eating cold leftovers the next day for lunch.

INGREDIENTS:

Canola oil or butter or Ghee	1 T
Cinnamon	1 3" stick
Cloves whole	5
Cashew nuts	⅓ Cup
Onion large, sliced	1
Raisins	⅓ Cup
Tomatoes fresh, diced	2
Jalapeño pepper chopped	1
Basmati rice rinse and soak 2-8 hrs	1 Cup
Water	2 Cups
Turmeric	1 t
Cardamom ground	½ t
Salt	½ t
Lentil sprouts	4 Cups
Cilantro chopped with tender stems	1 Cup

DIRECTIONS:

1. Assemble and prepare all ingredients.

2. Heat a 3-quart pan on medium-high with oil, cinnamon stick, cloves, cashews and onion; sauté 3-4 minutes.

3. Add raisins, tomatoes (reserve some for garnish) and jalapeño. Cook 1-2 minutes.

4. Add rice with its soaking water, turmeric, ground cardamom and salt.

5. Bring to a boil; cover and cook for 5 -7 minutes until half cooked.

6. Add sprouts and cilantro (reserve some for garnish); cook covered until tender.

7. Garnish with reserved tomato and cilantro.

8. Serve with raita (p. 49), kadhi (p. 59) or plain yogurt and a salad or vegetable.

NUTRITION INFORMATION PER SERVING:
Calories: 203 **Protein:** 7 g **Total carbohydrates:** 36 g
Fiber: 2 g **Total fat:** 5.5 g **Sodium:** 115 mg
Calcium: 25 mg **Omega-3 Fats (ALA):** 180 mg

Rice with Beans and Vegetables

Simple – One-dish / One-pot Meal – Serves 6

INGREDIENTS:

Brown rice	1 Cup
Water	1½ Cups
Lentils black or green	½ Cup
Water	1 Cup
Cumin seeds	¾ t
Cinnamon	1 3" stick
Cloves whole	6
Onion sliced	1
Olive oil	2 T
Tomato chopped	1
Cilantro chopped with tender stems	1 Cup
Garlic chopped	3 cloves
Ginger fresh or frozen, grated	1 t
Hot green pepper chopped	1
Almonds sliced	¼ Cup
Turmeric	½ t
Salt	to taste or ½ t
Vegetables assorted, cut, fresh or frozen	1 pound

DIRECTIONS:

1. Assemble and prepare all ingredients.

2. Combine tomato, cilantro, garlic, ginger, hot chili pepper, almonds, turmeric and salt.

3. Heat a 3-quart pan on medium-high with cumin seeds, cinnamon stick, cloves, oil and sliced onion; sauté for 3-5 minutes.

4. Add combined ingredients, lentils and rice with their soaking water; stir to mix; bring to a boil; if using fresh vegetables add them, stir and simmer covered; cook al dente.

5. If using frozen vegetables add them later when rice and beans are almost cooked.

6. Serve with a salad and raita (p. 49) or plain yogurt.

VARIATIONS & OPTIONS:

- For variety, speed and fragrance add garam masala (p. 133) in place of ginger, garlic and hot chili pepper.

- Substitute tomato paste, tomato or V-8 juice or puréed tomatoes for fresh tomato.

- Substitute canned beans for dry lentils and add them when rice is almost cooked.

- Substitute another herb for cilantro.

NUTRITION INFORMATION PER SERVING:
Calories: 269 **Protein:** 9 g **Total carbohydrates:** 41 g
Fiber: 9 g **Total fat:** 8 g **Sodium:** 120 mg
Calcium: 52 mg **Omega-3 Fats (ALA):** 0 mg

When cooking grains and beans, always cook extra to put in the freezer for a quick healthy meal you can put together with the suggestions that follow. The amount of mixed grains and beans and the proportion of the following ingredients may be adjusted according to your preference and taste. You can make up your own combination or use only one or some of the following ingredients for your hot cereal mixture.

Mix together any number of grains and beans in any proportion to suit your likes, dislikes and tolerance: quinoa, amaranth, barley, millet, brown rice, steel cut oats, buckwheat groats, black french lentils, green lentils, mung beans, red adzuki beans, corn grits, and soy grits.

I have, on occasion, dry-roasted each grain and bean separately, for 3-4 minutes, in a heavy pan – I use cast iron – on medium heat. The pan should be heated well before roasting the grains. Mix all the roasted or unroasted grains and beans together in a big container and allow them to cool completely before storing them. Store them in a sealed container in a cool dry place.

Soaking before you cook: If possible, soak the mixed grains and beans overnight, which will reduce your cooking time and fuel consumption. For every cup of mixed grains and beans add 2 ½ to 3-½ cups water. Add 3 cups or more water for a softer porridge like consistency. Cook in a pressure cooker, crock-pot, slow cooker, rice cooker or any other cooking method you choose.

The history of the breakfast mixed grains (we call this hot cereal) has evolved over the past 37 years, since my son Ram was 6 months old. When Ram was ready to start solid foods, I first introduced one grain, rice. It was cooked soft and pureed. Over time I cooked steel cut oats with rice, pureed them to a consistency similar to porridge. Soon after that he was introduced to a simple khichadi. Then I added millet, and the recipe evolved after Krupa was born, incorporating beans and other grains. Even today, at age 32, Krupa enjoys her hot cereal with butter and lemon or limejuice for any meal of the day – comfort food!

Krupa's Favorite Hot Cereal Mix

Simple – Mix grains to keep handy

INGREDIENTS:

Quinoa	2 Cups
Millet	1 Cup
Corn grits	1 Cup
Short grain brown rice	1 Cup
Steel cut oats	⅓ Cup
French lentils	⅓ Cup
Adzuki beans	⅓ Cup
Mung beans	⅓ Cup

DIRECTIONS:

Sort and scan through the dry grains and beans to remove any stones or sticks. Mix them together and store in a container for future use.

Krupa's Favorite Breakfast Hot Cereal

Simple – From the Mix above – Serves 4

INGREDIENTS:

Hot cereal mixed grains	1 Cup
Water	2 ½ to 3 Cups

DIRECTIONS:

1. The night or day before, soak 1 cup of hot cereal mixed grains in 2 ½ to 3 cups water; cook them with their soaking water in the morning by bringing to a boil, cover, reduce heat to low and cook to the consistency you like. Alternatively, the night before, cook previously soaked hot cereal mix in its soaking water, refrigerate and just reheat to save time in the morning rush. Krupa cooks them in a rice cooker, I use a pressure cooker.

2. Serve hot with butter, sprinkle with salt and lemon juice, my daughter's favorite.

3. Serve hot or cold with honey, fresh or dried fruit, nuts and/or a dash of cinnamon or nutmeg and milk; another of Krupa's favorite.

4. Cook hot cereal mix with water and dried fruit.

5. Cooked hot cereal may be stored in the refrigerator for up to 5 days; it freezes well.

NUTRITION INFORMATION PER SERVING:
Calories: 161 **Protein:** 6 g **Total carbohydrates:** 31 g
Fiber: 4 g **Total fat:** 1.5 g **Sodium:** 4 mg
Calcium: 20 mg **Omega-3 Fats (ALA):** 0 mg

VARIATIONS & OPTIONS:

Cooked Hot Cereal For Breakfast:

- Serve cooked grains and beans hot with butter, ghee or plain or herbed cream cheese.

- Serve cooked grains and beans cold or hot with milk, dairy or non-dairy, and any one or more of the following: honey, dried or fresh fruit, chopped nuts and a dash of cinnamon, cardamom or nutmeg.

Simple Options for other meals:

- Add to the cooked grains and beans some grated cheese and any one of the following: herbed or spiced oil, pesto sauce, pasta sauce or salsa. You can serve this cold in the summer (taking advantage of the resistant starch (p. 67-68)) and heated in the winter. Cooked grains and beans can be a side dish or served on a big salad as a one-dish meal.

- If you have frozen some cooked grains and beans, here's a quick meal idea. Make a soup by adding them to heated V-8 vegetable juice, carrot or tomato juice. Use the juices as your soup base; add cooked mixed grains and beans with herbs and spices of your choice.

- Miso paste can be used to make an instant broth for a soup base, to which you add fresh or frozen vegetables, herbs and spices plus the mixed grains and beans for a quick meal.

- Add herbs, spices and vegetables to cooked mixed grains and beans to make a cold salad similar to pasta salad to enjoy the benefits of resistant starch.

Stir-fried Hot Cereal

Simple – Serves 6

VARIATIONS & OPTIONS:

- Add ½ t grated ginger to this recipe.

- Add cayenne according to taste or substitute fresh ground black pepper or finely minced jalapeno for cayenne pepper.

- Add fresh or frozen vegetables in step 4 to make this a quick one-dish meal. Peas, corn or spinach would go well with the yogurt, but do not hesitate to experiment with other vegetables you have on hand and need to use up.

INGREDIENTS:

Cumin seeds	¼ t
Black mustard seeds	¼ t
Canola oil	4 t
Asafetida	pinch
Onion medium, chopped	1
Garlic chopped	2 cloves
Cooked (dry mix 1 Cup) leftover grains packed	3 Cups
Yogurt plain low fat, dairy or nondairy	1 Cup
Turmeric	¼ t
Cayenne pepper	⅛ t
Salt	¼ t
Cilantro chopped with tender stems, chopped	½ Cup
Tomato diced	1

DIRECTIONS:

1. Assemble and prepare all ingredients.

2. Heat cumin and mustard seeds in a 2-quart pan.

3. Before the seeds begin to pop, add oil, asafetida, onion and garlic. Stir-fry 2 to 3 minutes, till onion is tender and translucent.

4. Add cooked grains, yogurt, turmeric, cayenne and salt. Stir to mix well and cook till yogurt is well absorbed into the grains and grains are heated through.

5. Garnish with cilantro and tomato.

6. Use for a weekend lunch or serve for dinner with a salad or vegetable.

7. This tastes very good unheated, so enjoy the benefit of resistant starch (p. 67-68).

NUTRITION INFORMATION PER SERVING:
Calories: 173 **Protein:** 6 g **Total carbohydrates:** 27 g
Fiber: 3 g **Total fat:** 4.5 g **Sodium:** 84 mg
Calcium: 90 mg **Omega-3 Fats (ALA):** 280 mg

www.FeedingHealth.com

FLOURS

Gluten is a protein found in wheat, rye and barley; it is not found in oats. However, if oats are processed alongside wheat products, they may be "contaminated" with gluten. Based on Dr. Fasano's research 1% of the population may have celiac disease and non-celiac gluten sensitivity may affect 6% of the population. Individuals with celiac disease or with non-celiac gluten sensitivity are unable to eat foods containing gluten.

Traditionally, roti (also known as chapatti) and most all of the Indian flat breads are made from white whole-wheat flour also known as chapatti flour. Some rotis are made from other grain and bean flours such as bajri flour, ragi flour or corn flour or combination of these flours with wheat flour. So, for those who can tolerate wheat the first roti recipe uses wheat flour.

Plain Roti (Chapatti)

Simple – 6 Rotis

INGREDIENTS:

Water warm . . . . ⅓ Cup

Chapatti flour or **whole-wheat flour** (extra for rolling). . . . . 1 Cup

Oil olive (optional). . . . . .1 t

Butter (or ghee) optional for topping the 6 chapattis . . . . 1 T

DIRECTIONS:

1. Assemble and prepare all ingredients.

2. Rub oil into the flour with your fingers and add water; knead dough well, cover and allow resting for at least 10 minutes before rolling. Dough may be refrigerated or frozen for use at a later time.

3. Divide dough into 6 small round balls.

4. Take a ball of dough, roll it in flour and gently flatten it between your palms.

5. Roll the flattened disk in flour; with rolling pin gently roll dough out to 6" diameter.

6. In a hot heavy-bottomed skillet, dry roast the roti on both sides. If all goes well, it should puff up. Or – cook in a tortilla press; place the flattened ball of dough in the center of the heated tortilla press, press the top lid over the dough and before you know it you have a cooked flat roti. Google tortilla press and you will find plenty to select from. Several of my patients use them with great success.

7. Brush the roti on one side with ghee or butter if desired.

8. Serve with a vegetable or bean dish.

VARIATIONS & OPTIONS:

- Substitute milk for water to increase protein and calcium.

- Add dry milk powder to flour to increase protein and calcium.

- Add turmeric and ground cumin to flour and make dough.

- Add black pepper, turmeric and ground cumin to flour and make dough.

- Add grated zucchini to spices and make dough.

- Spread peanut butter or any nut butter with sliced bananas on the roti.

NUTRITION INFORMATION PER SERVING:
Calories: 73 **Protein:** 3 g **Total carbohydrates:** 14 g
Fiber: 2 g **Total fat:** 1 gram **Sodium:** 0 mg
Calcium: 0 mg **Omega-3 Fats (ALA):** 10 mg

Oat Flour Roti (Chapatti)

Simple – 6 Rotis

Oats, oat bran and oatmeal contain a fiber known as beta-glucan. Research shows that beta-glucan lowers cholesterol levels and has beneficial effects in diabetes. Avenanthramides are antioxidant compounds unique to oats. Antioxidants prevent free radicals from damaging LDL cholesterol, thus reducing the risk of cardiovascular disease. In addition to its fiber benefits, oats provide selenium, a necessary cofactor of the antioxidant glutathione peroxidase. Selenium works with vitamin E in many important antioxidant systems throughout the body.[9]

INGREDIENTS:

Oat flour (extra for rolling) . . . . 1 Cup
Olive oil. . . . . .2 t
Water . . . . ⅓ Cup
Butter (or ghee optional) for topping the 6 chapattis . . . . 1 T

DIRECTIONS:

1. Assemble and prepare all ingredients.
2. Rub oil into the flour with your fingers; add ¼ cup water and mix to make dough. Add remaining water as needed.
3. Knead dough until it is smooth and does not stick to the fingers; cover dough; let it rest at least 10 minutes. Dough may be refrigerated or frozen for use at a later time.
4. Divide dough into 6 small balls; flatten each ball between your palms.
5. Roll the flattened disk in flour and with rolling pin roll dough out to 6" diameter.
6. Heat a cast-iron or other heavy-bottomed skillet or griddle on medium-high heat while you roll the dough out.
7. Cook the roti on both sides in the hot skillet. If all goes well it should puff up.
8. When cooked, remove from pan and brush one side with ghee or butter.
9. Serve with a vegetable or beans as part of a meal.

VARIATIONS & OPTIONS:

- Flatten the roti in a tortilla press for ease and convenience.

- Add ¼ t salt (or less) if you like.

- Substitute any other flour for the oat flour – corn, buckwheat, millet or soy or use any combination of flours, such as ¾ cup oat flour with ¼ cup soy flour. The amount of water needed may vary depending on the flour you use.

- Instead of water use milk, dairy or non-dairy, to make dough.

- The dough will keep in the refrigerator for several days and you can also freeze it.

- Very finely grated zucchini, beets or carrots can be added to the flour to make dough: To the flour add a little salt, turmeric, ground cumin, cayenne, little yogurt and the vegetable; mix well, add water, make dough and continue with the basic recipe.

NUTRITION INFORMATION PER SERVING:
Calories: 65 **Protein:** 2 g **Total carbohydrates:** 9 g
Fiber: 1 gram **Total fat:** 2.5 g **Sodium:** 1 mg
Calcium: 0 mg **Omega-3 Fats (ALA):** 10 mg

Spinach Roti (Chapatti)

Elaborate – Makes 12 Rotis

In traditional Chinese and Ayurvedic medicine, turmeric has been used to support digestion and liver function, relieve arthritis pain and to regulate menstruation. Turmeric, rich in potassium and iron, contains a chemical called curcumin, which has antioxidant, anti-cancer and anti-inflammatory properties. Its pungent, bitter and slightly astringent properties stimulate those taste buds. Ginger provides anti-inflammatory benefits. According to Ayurveda cumin seeds aid digestion and balance all three doshas.[8,9,12]

INGREDIENTS:

Oat flour (or **wheat**) . . . . .2 Cups
Olive oil . . . . 2 T
Turmeric . . . . ¼ t
Cumin ground . . . . .1 t
Salt . . . . ½ t
Ginger fresh or frozen, grated. . . . . ½ t
Garlic minced . . . . ½ t
Cayenne or **chili pepper** ground . . . . ½ t
Spinach fresh 3 Cups, finely minced or processed . . . . ½ Cup
Water . . . . ⅔ to ¾ Cup
Butter (or ghee) for topping the 12 rotis. . . . . 2 T

DIRECTIONS:

1. Assemble and prepare all ingredients.
2. Except for water and butter, mix all ingredients together well.
3. Add water little at a time to make stiff dough.
4. Knead the dough well, cover and let it rest 10 to 15 minutes.
5. Divide dough into 12 small balls; roll each ball between your palms and flatten.
6. Heat a cast iron or other heavy-bottomed skillet on medium-high while you roll the dough out. You could also make them in a tortilla press.
7. Roll the flattened disk in flour; with rolling pin gently roll it out to 6" in diameter.
8. Cook the roti on both sides on a hot skillet. It should puff up if all goes well.
9. Brush the hot roti with ghee or butter.
10. Serve with a meal or enjoy as a snack.

VARIATIONS & OPTIONS:

- Substitute any other dark green leafy vegetable for spinach.

- Substitute parsley, cilantro or another herb for spinach.

- Substitute grated zucchini for spinach.

NUTRITION INFORMATION PER SERVING:
Calories: 90 **Protein:** 2 g **Total carbohydrates:** 5 g
Fiber: 1 gram **Total fat:** 2 g **Sodium:** 53 mg
Calcium: 10 mg **Omega-3 Fats (ALA):** 0 mg

Upma

Simple – Serves 6

Traditionally upma is made with a coarsely ground wheat flour; texture is similar to cream of wheat. I am using whole-grain brown cream of rice to make it gluten free (p. 103).

(p. 103)

VARIATIONS & OPTIONS:

- Substitute quinoa, amaranth, steel cut oats, millet, corn, soy or oat grits or a combination of soy, oat and corn grits for brown cream of rice.

- Substitute any other vegetable for the green peas – such as edamame, corn, green beans, peas and carrots.

- Plain yogurt may be added in step 6 of this recipe; just substitute yogurt for part of the water.

INGREDIENTS:

Black mustard seeds . . . . ½ t
Urad daal (optional) . . . . ½ t
Asafetida. . . . . pinch
Onion medium, thinly sliced. 1
Jalapeño or **hot green chili pepper** slit in half 1
Curry leaves (limbdo, optional) . . . . 6 to 7
Canola oil . . . . .4 t
Brown cream of rice, uncooked. . . . . 1 Cup
Water . . . . .2 ¼ Cups
Salt . . . . to taste or ¼ t
Turmeric. . . . . ½ t
Green peas fresh or frozen. . . . . 1 Cup
Cilantro chopped with tender stems . . . . .½ Cup
Lemon or **limejuice**. . . . . to taste

DIRECTIONS:

1. Assemble and prepare all ingredients.
2. Heat a 2-quart skillet or pan with mustard seeds and urad daal.
3. When the urad daal gets slightly toasted and pink add asafetida, onion, curry leaves, and jalapeño. If using fresh peas add them at this point.
4. Stir, add oil and sauté for 2 minutes on medium-high heat.
5. Add cream of rice and sauté for about 1 minute.
6. Add water, turmeric and salt to taste.
7. Stir, bring to a boil, reduce heat and cook covered until all the water is absorbed.
8. If using frozen peas add them now and stir to combine.
9. Add cilantro and lemon juice to taste.
10. This makes a good lunch served with plain yogurt or raita (p. 49). It may also be served with a meal as a side dish.

NUTRITION INFORMATION PER SERVING:
Calories: 162 **Protein:** 3 g **Total carbohydrates:** 29 g
Fiber: 2 g **Total fat:** 3.5 g **Sodium:** 50 mg
Calcium: 21 mg **Omega-3 Fats (ALA):** 310 mg

Steamed Rice Flour Dumplings – Papadi No Lote

Simple – Serves 4

Traditionally the steamed rice flour papadi is rolled out and dried in the sun, similar to the legume-flour papadams (papads) available in Indian stores. The dried papadi is generally toasted or occasionally fried in oil for special feasts. This steamed dough is my family's (mine too) favorite to snack on or eat any time of the day. I still make this each time Ram and Krupa come home. In Gujarat, it is usually eaten with a little good cold-pressed sesame or peanut oil.

INGREDIENTS:

Brown rice flour	1 Cup
Baking soda	¼ t
Water	1½ Cups
Salt	¼ t
Cloves ground	¼ t
Sesame seeds	1 T
Ajwain seeds	½ t
Black pepper ground, and/or **hot green chili** minced	½ t
Olive oil	4 t

DIRECTIONS:

1. Assemble and prepare all ingredients.

2. Combine rice flour with the baking soda; set aside.

3. In a 2-quart pan combine water with salt, cloves, sesame seeds, ajwain seeds and either hot green chili and/or black pepper. Bring water to a boil.

4. Add flour with baking soda to the boiling water; turn heat off and stir the flour into the water with the back of a wooden spoon in a circular motion to prevent lumps of dry flour.

5. Cover tightly and keep on the stove top, with heat off, at least 15 minutes or until cool enough to handle.

6. Knead dough to make it smooth and break up any dry flour lumps that may be left. You may need to grease your palms with a little oil.

7. Form small patties or pones and steam for 7 minutes either in a steamer lined with cheesecloth or covered in the microwave.

8. Serve with a drizzle of good cold-pressed oil.

VARIATIONS & OPTIONS:

- Substitute 6 whole cloves for ground cloves.

- Add ½ t cumin seeds in the water.

- Substitute oat flour (or rolled oats) or coarsely ground corn flour (corn grits) for rice flour in this recipe.

- Try a combination of flours – coarse ground corn flour with either brown rice flour or rolled oats.

NUTRITION INFORMATION PER SERVING:
Calories: 164 **Protein:** 3 g **Total carbohydrates:** 24 g
Fiber: 1 gram **Total fat:** 7 g **Sodium:** 146 mg
Calcium: 24 mg **Omega-3 Fats (ALA):** 0 mg

Bean & Grain Flours

These savory pancakes (puda) can very easily be a quick meal when enjoyed with a salad, soup or vegetable. They can be made with single bean flour such as chickpea flour, soy flour or mung bean flour or mixture of different grains and bean flours combined with vegetables, herbs and spices. Often yogurt is added to the batter. If you do not have the flours, you can make a batter from soaked beans and grains. Recipe follows (p. 112). To the batter add vegetables, herbs and spices and fry them on a skillet as you would pancakes. The batter freezes well, so be sure to plan for the freezer. Try alone or with any combinations of the following flours: soy, rice, buckwheat, oat, millet, barley, almond, mung bean, urad and chickpea. Here are a few different ways to cook them.

Chick Pea Flour Puda (Pancakes)

Simple – Makes 10 Puda

INGREDIENTS:

Chickpea flour (besan)	2 Cups
Canola oil for frying	5 T
Salt	to taste or ½ t
Turmeric	1 t
Ajwain seeds	1 t
Cayenne or **black pepper**	to taste or ½ t
Onion minced	½ Cup
Cilantro chopped with tender stems	2 Cups
Water	2 ¼ Cups

DIRECTIONS:

1. Assemble and prepare all ingredients.
2. Combine chickpea flour with salt, turmeric, ajwain, cayenne, onion and cilantro; add water to make batter.
3. Allow batter to rest for 15 minutes.
4. Preheat a cast iron skillet on medium-high. Spread a little oil on the skillet; add ¼ cup of batter; tilt the skillet to distribute batter evenly. Turn heat to medium and cover the skillet.
5. Cook the puda until it browns around the edges and sets on top, 2 to 3 minutes.
6. Turn puda over with a spatula and cook for 1 minute longer.
7. Keep the puda warm in a pre-heated oven while you finish making all of them.
8. Enjoy as part of a meal with vegetables, soup or salad.

NUTRITION INFORMATION PER SERVING:
Calories: 118 **Protein:** 4 g **Total carbohydrates:** 12 g
Fiber: 2 g **Total fat:** 6 g **Sodium:** 70 mg
Calcium: 13 mg **Omega-3 Fats (ALA):** 0 mg

VARIATIONS & OPTIONS:
- Substitute parsley or dill to taste for cilantro.
- Substitute buckwheat or soy flour for chickpea flour.
- Substitute scallions or chives for onion.
- Add fresh chopped spinach to the batter.
- Substitute oregano or cumin seeds for ajwain seeds.

Mixed-Grain Bean Flour Puda (Pancakes)

Simple – Makes 10 Puda

VARIATIONS & OPTIONS:

- Substitute 2 cups chopped scallions for the large onion.

- Substitute 2 to 3 cups finely chopped parsley for cilantro.

- Add 1 to 2 T ground flax seeds.

- Add chopped fresh or frozen spinach or other dark green leafy vegetables.

- Add grated zucchini, carrots or yellow squash to the batter.

- Substitute 2 cups of any combination of these flours – chickpea, mung bean, soy, coarsely ground corn, buckwheat, barley, oat, rice and/or almond flour.

INGREDIENTS:

Soy, chickpea, brown rice & oat flour . ½ Cup each, total 2 Cups
Turmeric . . . . ¾ t
Salt . . . . to taste or ½ t
Ajwain seeds . . . . 1 t
Ginger fresh or frozen, grated . . . . 1 t
Garlic minced . . . . 1 t
Jalapeño pepper minced . . . . 1 t
Onion large, minced 1
Cilantro chopped with tender stems . . . . .2 Cups
Yogurt low fat, plain, dairy or non-dairy . . . . 1 Cup
Water . . . . 1 Cup
   as needed to make batter's consistency similar to pancake batter
Canola oil for frying . . . . 5 T

DIRECTIONS:

1. Assemble and prepare all ingredients.

2. Combine the flours with turmeric, salt, ajwain seeds, ginger, garlic, jalapeño, cilantro and onion; mix well and add yogurt and mix again.

3. Add water as needed to make pancake like batter.

4. Allow batter to rest for 10 to 15 minutes. Make puda or set the mixture aside for an hour or even overnight in the refrigerator for use later.

5. Preheat a cast iron or other heavy-bottomed skillet on medium-high. Spread a little oil on the skillet; add ¼ cup of batter; tilt the skillet to distribute it evenly.

6. Turn heat to medium; cover the skillet. Cook puda until browned around the edges and set on top – 2 to 3 minutes.

7. Turn puda over with a spatula and cook it for 1 to 2 minutes longer.

8. Keep puda warm in a pre-heated oven while you finish making all of them.

9. Enjoy as part of a meal with a vegetable, soup or salad.

NUTRITION INFORMATION PER SERVING:
Calories: 138 **Protein:** 4 g **Total carbohydrates:** 15 g
Fiber: 2 g **Total fat:** 7 g **Sodium:** 62 mg
Calcium: 12 mg **Omega-3 Fats (ALA):** 0 mg

Soaked Grains and Beans Puda (Pancakes)

Elaborate – Makes 12 Puda

INGREDIENTS:

Brown rice soak 12 to 24 hrs . . . . ½ Cup
Whole or **split mung beans** soak 12 to 24 hrs . . . . ½ Cup
Lentils soak 12 to 24 hrs . . . . ½ Cup
Channa daal soak 12 to 24 hrs . . . . ½ Cup
Tuver daal soak 12 to 24 hrs . . . . ½ Cup
Water . . . . 1 ½ to 2 Cups
Hot green chilies or **jalapeños** . . . . according to taste or 2
Ginger fresh. . . . . 2" piece
Onions or **scallions** chopped . . . . .2 Cups
Yogurt (dairy or non-dairy) plain, low-fat . . . . ½ Cup
Turmeric . . . . 1 t
Salt . . . . to taste or ¾ t
Cilantro chopped with tender stems . . . . .2 Cups
Canola oil for frying . . . . 5 T
Black mustard seeds . . . . .1 t
Urad daal (optional) . . . . .1 t
Curry leaves (optional). . . . . 8 to 10

DIRECTIONS:

1. Assemble and prepare all ingredients.
2. Grind soaked grains with hot green chilies, ginger, onions, yogurt, water, turmeric and salt to a batter consistency. Add more water if needed.
3. Add chopped cilantro and mix well.
4. Do vaghar of mustard seeds, urad daal, curry leaves and asafetida in oil; add this seasoned oil to the batter, stirring well to mix.
5. Let batter rest for 15 minutes.
6. Preheat a seasoned cast iron or a heavy-bottomed skillet on medium-high. Spread a little oil on the skillet; add ¼ cup of batter; tilt the skillet to distribute it evenly.
7. Turn heat to medium and cover the skillet. Cook the puda until browned around the edges and set on top – 2 to 3 minutes.
8. Turn puda over with a spatula and cook 2 minutes longer.
9. Keep puda warm in a pre-heated oven while you finish making all of them.
10. The batter can stay in the refrigerator for several days or you can freeze it.

NUTRITION INFORMATION PER SERVING:

Calories: 184 **Protein:** 9 g **Total carbohydrates:** 27 g
Fiber: 7 g **Total fat:** 5 g **Sodium:** 86 mg
Calcium: 67 mg **Omega-3 Fats (ALA):** 0 mg

VARIATIONS & OPTIONS:

- Substitute or add millet, quinoa, barley or corn grits in place of brown rice.

- Use a combination of ½ cup each of rice, millet, lentils, mung beans and adzuki beans, and proceed according to directions.

- Substitute split yellow and green peas for the channa daal and tuver daal.

- Add 6 to 8 cups fresh spinach or any other dark green leafy vegetable and process with onions and grains to make batter.

- Add 2 T ground flax seeds to the grains and beans before grinding.

- Substitute parsley or mint for cilantro.

- Substitute garlic for onion or use both.

- Add ½ cup oat flour to the batter and adjust the spices to taste.

- A Simple alternative is to bake this batter instead of frying the puda (pancakes). If planning to bake, keep batter fairly firm. Do not add too much water or if you need to thicken the batter, add oat flour. Add ½ t of baking powder to the batter, mix well and bake in a preheated oven at 375°F for 45 – 60 minutes, depending on the size of the baking dish; or bake them in muffin pans for 50 minutes or until set.

Muthia

Elaborate – Serves 8

INGREDIENTS:

Chickpea flour (besan) . . . . 1 Cup
Cornmeal . . . . ½ Cup
Cream of brown rice . . . . ½ Cup
Salt . . . . ¾ t
Baking powder . . . . ½ t
Ajwain . . . . 1 t
Turmeric . . . . 1 t
Coconut unsweetened, grated (reserve some for garnish) . . . . . 3 T
Cilantro chopped with tender stems . . . . 2 Cups
  (reserve some for garnish)
Yogurt low fat, dairy or non-dairy, plain. . . . . ½ Cup
Ginger fresh or frozen, grated. . . . . 1 ½ t
Garlic chopped . . . . 5 cloves
Jalapeño pepper minced, to taste or 1
Spinach very finely minced . . . . 5 Cups
Water if needed . . . . ¼ Cup
Lemon or **lime**, juiced . . . . to taste
Vaghar ingredients for step 7 below:
Canola oil . . . . 2 T
Mustard seeds black . . . . ¾ t
Sesame seeds . . . . ¼ Cup
Asafetida . . . . a pinch

DIRECTIONS:

1. Assemble and prepare all ingredients.
2. Mix flours together.
3. Add salt, baking powder, ajwain seeds, turmeric and coconut. Mix well.
4. Add cilantro, yogurt, ginger, garlic, jalapeno and spinach; mix well to form soft dough adding ¼ cup or less water if needed.
5. Lubricate your hands with water and scoop up half-cups of dough, forming small pones 3 ½" long by 1 ½" wide.
6. Put pones in an ungreased steamer pan and steam them for 45 minutes. Allow steam to cool off a little, 15 – 20 minutes, before opening the steamer lid.
7. Serve pones hot with a vaghar poured over them and garnished with coconut and chopped cilantro plus a squirt of lemon or limejuice.

To do the vaghar:
- Heat mustard seeds in a small skillet.
- When seeds change color and before they start popping, add oil and asafetida.
- Turn heat off and add sesame seeds. Pour the vaghar over the cooked muthia pones; garnish with coconut, cilantro and lemon or limejuice.

8 Serve hot or cold with or without raita.

NUTRITION INFORMATION PER SERVING:
Calories: 198 **Protein:** 6 g **Total carbohydrates:** 26 g
Fiber: 4 g **Total fat:** 8 g **Sodium:** 176 mg
Calcium: 108 mg **Omega-3 Fats (ALA):** 310 mg

Zucchini Corn Muthia Muffins

Simple – Serves 12

INGREDIENTS:

Rolled oats	½ Cup
Oat bran	⅓ Cup
Brown rice flour	⅓ Cup
Whole soy flour	⅓ Cup
Salt	½ t
Turmeric	1 t
Olive oil	2 T
Ginger fresh	½" piece
Garlic minced	4 cloves
Jalapeño or **other hot green chili pepper**	½
Zucchini grated	2 Cups
Corn kernels fresh or frozen, puréed	1½ Cups
Cilantro chopped with tender stems	2 Cups
Lime juiced	1
Water	¼ Cup

DIRECTIONS:

1. Assemble and prepare all ingredients.

2. Combine olive oil with rolled oats, oat bran, rice flour, soy flour, salt and turmeric. Rub oil well into flour mixture.

3. Either grate these ingredients by hand or use this method: In a food processor chop garlic, ginger and jalapeño for a few seconds. Add big cut pieces of zucchini and pulse for a few seconds to chop them fine. Add cilantro and pulse a few seconds. Add corn and pulse a few seconds. The mixture should look finely chopped.

4. Add limejuice and water to the vegetables; mix and stir into the flour mixture.

5. Preheat the oven to 500°F.

6. Spray a 12- or 24-muffin tray with oil or use muffin papers.

7. Fill muffin cups with batter; turn oven to 400°F; place tray on the middle rack of the oven; bake at 400°F for 5 minutes. Turn oven down to 375°F and bake for another 35 minutes.

8. Enjoy these muffins for snack or with a meal. Cooled, unheated muffins provide the benefit of resistant starch (p. 67-68).

9. These muthia muffins freeze well.

NUTRITION INFORMATION PER SERVING:
Calories: 97 **Protein:** 3 g **Total carbohydrates:** 15 g
Fiber: 2 g **Total fat:** 4 g **Sodium:** 51 mg
Calcium: 17 mg **Omega-3 Fats (ALA):** 10 mg

VARIATIONS & OPTIONS:

- Substitute any other vegetable for the zucchini.

- Substitute any other combinations of flours.

- We enjoy spinach, corn and walnut combination.

- Substitute any other dark green leafy vegetable for the spinach.

- Add grated cheese to the batter.

Most of us like fruits: they make excellent snack foods and desserts. They are colorful, sweet and relatively low in calories. About 80% to 95% of fruit is water. Fruits provide fiber, phytonutrients and minerals such as iron and potassium, small amounts of calcium and magnesium, as well as vitamins such as vitamin C, folate and beta-carotene. With the exception of avocado, fruits contain little or no fat and no cholesterol.[8,9]

Although they are fruits, avocados have a high fat content; ranging from 71% to 88% of their total calories, which is about 20 times the average for other fruits. A typical avocado contains 30 grams of fat; however, 20 of these fat grams are health-promoting monounsaturated fats such as alpha-linolenic acid (an omega-3 fatty acid) and oleic acid.[8,9]

Among fruits, avocados are the richest source of lutein, alpha and gamma tocopherols and beta-carotene. They also contain small amounts of zeaxanthin and cryptoxanthin, along with other carotenoids, phytosterols, chlorophyll, polyphenols and glutathione. The carotenoids are concentrated just beneath the peel. Carotenoids are fat-soluble, so the fat in the avocado helps in their absorption. Lutein, the major antioxidant in avocados, accumulates in the macular region of the human retina. This may help prevent macular degeneration, which is the most common cause of blindness in Americans over 65. Avocados contain a variety of phytonutrients, fiber and vitamins such as B6, C, K and folate plus minerals such as copper and potassium.[8,9,10]

You will notice my liberal use lime or lemon juice in the recipes. Besides the fact that I enjoy the fresh taste, limes and lemons contain high proportions of alkaline-forming elements and supply vitamin C, which allows for better absorption of minerals such as iron and calcium from plant foods. Despite their acid flavor, citrus fruits form alkaline residues. When an alkaline environment is maintained in the body, metabolic, enzymatic, immunologic and repair mechanisms function at their best. Most vegetables and fruits contain higher proportions of alkaline-forming elements than other foods. High fat, high protein animal foods, on the other hand, generate acid-forming metabolites.[5,6,8,9]

People with diabetes can take advantage of avocado's healthful fat and nutrients by eating it with other fruits and in salads. Recipes using avocado are on pages 81 and 82.

Cranberry, Apple and Orange Relish

Simple – Makes 5 cups, 15 Servings

The phytonutrients in cranberries are phenolic acids, proanthocyanidins, anthocyanins, flavonoids and triterpenoids. They provide antioxidant, anti-inflammatory and anti-cancer benefits. Antioxidants are essential for optimum health and to combat free radicals that can damage cellular structures as well as DNA. Research indicates that cranberry's ability to provide urinary tract infection benefits is not primarily related to its acidity, but rather to its proanthocyanidin (PAC) content. The PACs in cranberry have a structure that makes it more difficult for certain types of bacteria to latch on to our urinary tract linings.[9]

This recipe is from my daughter Krupa. We use it for more than just Thanksgiving dinner. It is simple and delicious.

INGREDIENTS:

Cranberries fresh, organic . . . . 1 lb
Orange organic, unpeeled, quartered 1
Apples organic, cored, cut in big pieces 2
Honey . . . . ¼ Cup

DIRECTIONS:

1. Assemble and prepare all ingredients.
2. Pulse the orange in the food processor first. Then add apples and cranberries and process until all the fruit is crushed.
3. Add ¼ cup honey to the crushed fruit and mix well.

VARIATIONS & OPTIONS:

- Substitute maple syrup for honey.

- Make cranberry salsa by adding the following to 2 cups of the relish:
  - Jalapeño or other hot pepper... 1
  - Cilantro with tender stems, chopped... 4 cups
  - Cumin seeds, roasted, ground... ½ t (p. 132)
  - Salt to taste or... ¼ t
  - Pulse these ingredients together in a food processor and add to 2 cups of relish.
  - Serve with chips, crackers, sliced zucchini or cucumber, over beans, cooked leftover grains or baked potato.

- You can stir either the relish or salsa into cooked rice, millet, quinoa, amaranth, potatoes, or cooked white cannellini beans. Serve hot or cold.

- I enjoy the leftover sweet relish on plain yogurt for a snack.

- Use as a cranberry relish for Thanksgiving dinner.

NUTRITION INFORMATION PER SERVING:
Calories: 51 **Protein:** 0 g **Total carbohydrates:** 13 g
Fiber: 3 g **Total fat:** 0 g **Sodium:** 8 mg
Calcium: 12 mg **Omega-3 Fats (ALA):** 0 mg

When you are short on time, one-pot recipes provide hot, hearty meals without leaving many pots to clean after the meal. They can be healthy and nutritionally balanced. My family's favorite khichadi comes in handy as a one-dish meal. Use just one pot to make any version of khichadi with vegetables, herbs, nuts or seeds, adding a few simple spices or garam masala to make it fragrant and complete.

SIMPLE ONE-DISH MEAL IDEAS

1. For a one-pot one-dish meal in a bowl, cook the following ingredients together in any combination of your choice. For a stew or quick soup use miso for the broth. Eat this dish with raita or yogurt on the side, non-dairy or dairy.

   Grain, such as rice, millet or quinoa

   Canned beans, split beans, lentils, tofu, tempeh or frozen edamame

   Vegetables such as dark green leafy vegetables, tomatoes or any frozen vegetable

   Canned tomatoes, tomato paste, juice or puree or V-8 vegetable juice

   Flavor enhancer such as onion, garlic, ginger or hot green chilies

   Herbs such as cilantro, parsley, dill or tarragon

   Spices such as cumin, mustard, turmeric, cinnamon, cloves or garam masala

   Nuts and seeds such as sesame seeds, almonds, cashews or sunflower seeds

2. Build a salad for a one-dish meal. A variety of vegetables, some beans, cooked grains (Krupa's hot cereal mix) and fruit can add health-promoting phytonutrients, flavor and appeal to your meals. Use any combination of ingredients listed below. Buy or harvest high-quality and fresh ingredients and toss them together with your favorite dressing just before serving.

   Mixed greens – spinach, romaine, red leaf, watercress or mesclun.

   Add color – with tomato, broccoli florets, grated carrots, green or red peppers, beets, cauliflower or edible flowers.

   Sweeten with fruit – pineapple, pears, orange segments, sliced strawberries, cut apples or dried fruit. I like papaya, mango or grapefruit and avocado in combination.

   Add protein with tofu, canned beans, quinoa or edamame.

   Add a starch – cooked barley, brown rice or millet.

   Add a crunch with toasted sesame seeds, sunflower or pumpkin seeds, almonds, pecans, pistachios, pine nuts, walnuts or peanuts.

   Flavor with herbs – tarragon, chives, parsley, cilantro, marjoram, basil, thyme or mint.

   Dress salads with olive oil and balsamic vinegar or your favorite low fat dressing.

It's 5:30 pm – Soups & One-Dish Meals

Chickpea Stew

Simple – Serves 8

Rosemary grows on a small evergreen shrub and belongs to the Labiatae family that is related to mint. Its memorable flavor pairs well with garlic and chickpeas in this stew. Fresh rosemary is available throughout the year so choose fresh rosemary over the dried form of the herb since it is far superior in flavor.

INGREDIENTS:

Chickpeas boiled home cooked . . . . .4 Cups

Water for cooking chickpeas . . . . .3 Cups

Rosemary fresh (or dried 1 t) . . . . 2 T

Turmeric . . . . .1 t

Olive oil . . . . 2 T

Garlic minced . . . . .4 cloves

Onion chopped. 1

Hot green chili or **jalapeño** chopped . . . . to taste

Salt . . . . to taste or ½ t

Tomato paste (or 2 Cups tomato purée) . . . . 1 small can

Water to mix with tomato paste 10oz

Quinoa rinsed, drained . . . . 1 Cup

Water . . . . .3 Cups

Back pepper freshly ground . . . . to taste

DIRECTIONS:

1. Assemble and prepare all ingredients.

2. Cook soaked (12 – 24 hours) and rinsed chickpeas in 3 cups water, turmeric and rosemary; add salt and tomato paste mixed with water or tomato purée; set aside.

3. Heat olive oil in a large pot with garlic, onion and green chili; sauté 3-5 minutes.

4. Stir in cooked chickpea mixture with the cooking water.

5. Add quinoa with 3 cups water; cook until quinoa is tender (al dente).

6. Add black pepper to taste.

7. Serve hot with gluten free bread or muffins and salad.

VARIATIONS & OPTIONS:

- Substitute any other bean, pea or legume for chickpeas.

- Add more herbs to the soup according to taste preference.

- The stew freezes well so make extra to freeze for another meal.

- Add baby spinach, kale or any other dark green leafy vegetable to the soup. Cook until the spinach is wilted or kale is tender.

NUTRITION INFORMATION PER SERVING:
Calories: 247 **Protein:** 10 g **Total carbohydrates:** 39 g
Fiber: 9 g **Total fat:** 6 g **Sodium:** 104 mg
Calcium: 72 mg **Omega-3 Fats (ALA):** 0 mg

Spinach Soup

Simple – Serves 6

Spinach supplies over 50% of calories from protein. Spinach is an excellent source of carotenoids, folic acid, potassium, iron and calcium, in addition to its phytochemicals. Parsley provides vitamins A, C, K and folate, iron and flavonoids.[8,9,10]

INGREDIENTS:

Onions large, chopped 2
Olive oil . . . . 2 T
Spinach fresh, baby . . . . 1 pound
Water . . . . 3 Cups
Parsley with tender stems, minced . . . . ½ lb
Salt . . . . to taste or ¼ t
Lemon pepper . . . . to taste

DIRECTIONS:

1. Assemble and prepare all ingredients.
2. Sauté the onions in olive oil for a few minutes until they are tender.
3. Add spinach, stir and cook 2 to 3 minutes.
4. Add 2 cups water and parsley stir and bring to a boil; then turn heat off.
5. When cooled enough to handle purée in a blender; return soup to the pot.
6. Add remaining water, salt and pepper to taste.
7. If you like the soup thinner, add more water. Adjust salt and pepper to taste.
8. Serve the soup with gluten free bread, as part of a meal or with Krupa's hot cereal.

VARIATIONS & OPTIONS:

- Substitute any other dark green leafy vegetable for spinach.

- Substitute any other herb, such as cilantro, for parsley.

- Add a fruit to the dark green leafy vegetable in this recipe. For example, in the fall I have added cranberries in step 4 of the recipe to give this soup a different flavor and additional antioxidant benefits. The taste is good, however, the color changes from a bright green to a reddish green.

- Once I had a third of a head of Savoy cabbage that I wanted to use up and did not have parsley, so I modified this recipe: I added 1 t cumin seeds in step 2 with the onions; added 4 cups of shredded Savoy cabbage with spinach in step 3; adding a few minutes to the cooking time. I substituted cilantro for parsley in step 4. This turned out to be a tasty way to combine cruciferous vegetables with dark green leafy vegetables.

- Add cut grilled tempeh or tofu cubes to the soup before serving. Adjust salt and pepper to taste.

- Top the soup with whipped silken tofu, swirling it on top as a garnish. This adds more protein. Adjust salt and pepper to taste.

NUTRITION INFORMATION PER SERVING:
Calories: 91 **Protein:** 4 g **Total carbohydrates:** 10 g
Fiber: 4 g **Total fat:** 5 g **Sodium:** 130 mg
Calcium: 139 mg **Omega-3 Fats (ALA):** 0 mg

Red Pepper Soup

Simple – Serves 6

Onions supply vitamins B6, C and folate; and minerals such as chromium, manganese, molybdenum, potassium, phosphorus and copper. They are low in calories and have high polyphenol content and a large amount of quercetin. The flavonoids in onion are concentrated in the outer layers of the flesh. Peel off as little of the fleshy, edible portion as possible when removing the onion's outermost paper layer. Even a small amount of "over peeling" can result in loss of flavonoids. For example, a red onion can lose about 20% of its quercetin and almost 75% of its anthocyanins if it is "over peeled".[8,9,10] This recipe is from my niece, Kamini.

INGREDIENTS:

Red sweet peppers diced . . . . 2 lb
Onions large chopped. 2
Garlic chopped . . . . 4 cloves
Water . . . . .6 Cups
Olive oil. . . . . 1 T
Salt . . . . to taste
Lemon pepper . . . . to taste

DIRECTIONS:

1. Assemble and prepare all ingredients.

2. In a 3-quart pot add vegetables with 4 cups water; bring to a boil; cook until vegetables are tender.

3. When cooled enough to handle purée in a blender adding the remaining 2 cups of water; return soup to the pot.

4. Add olive oil, salt and lemon pepper to taste just before serving.

5. Serve as a meal with Krupa's hot cereal, bread or muffins.

VARIATIONS & OPTIONS:

- Add the zest of half a lemon to the vegetables while they are cooking. Add lemon juice to the soup after it has been puréed.

- Add ¼ cup of ground cashews, walnuts or almonds to soup before puréeing.

- Stir 2 T of any nut or seed butter into the soup after it has been puréed.

- Substitute carrots or any other vegetable for red peppers.

- Use either onion or garlic in the soup.

- Substitute leeks for onion and garlic.

- Add cooked or canned beans after puréeing the soup. Adjust amount of water added to desired consistency.

- Top with whipped silken tofu or swirl it into the soup before serving.

- Add small cubes of tofu to the soup for additional protein. Adjust salt and pepper to taste.

NUTRITION INFORMATION PER SERVING:
Calories: 84 **Protein:** 2 g **Total carbohydrates:** 13 g
Fiber: 4 g **Total fat:** 3 g **Sodium:** 55 mg
Calcium: 23 mg **Omega-3 Fats (ALA):** 0 mg

Meal Suggestions, including Gluten-free & Vegan Options

Individuals following a vegan diet may substitute non-dairy products for dairy products.

BREAKFAST FOODS

1. Make hot cereal with ⅓ cup oats, barley, millet or quinoa and add cinnamon, nutmeg, fresh or dried fruit or applesauce and 2 T nuts or seeds.

2. Serve cold whole-grain cereals or granola topped with fruit and milk or yogurt.

3. To a hot or cold cereal dish made with ⅓ cup oat bran or rice bran using milk or water for hot cereal, add fruit plus 2 T chopped walnuts or almonds or sesame seeds, 1 T ground flax seeds, cinnamon, and milk.

4. To whole grain cold cereals add 1 T ground flax seeds, 2 T chopped walnuts or almonds or sesame seeds, milk, fruit, and cinnamon.

5. Spread toast or a tortilla with almond, peanut, cashew, sunflower, pistachio, sesame, or hazelnut butter, top with sliced banana or other fruit, and eat with yogurt or a glass of milk.

6. Make a "hot or cold bean cereal" out of cooked adzuki or mung beans plus milk and fruit to sweeten – or whiz it all into a smoothie.

7. Combine cooked mixed grains with nuts or nut butter, milk and fruit.

8. Hot cereals can be cooked with water, juice or milk, sprinkled with cinnamon, cardamom or nutmeg, and topped with fruit and nuts.

9. Cook grits or polenta in water using millet, quinoa or corn grits seasoned with whatever herbs and spices you like.

10. Serve leftovers, cold or reheated.

11. Try sliced apple or banana with a dollop of nut butter such as almond, peanut, cashew, sunflower, soy, hazelnut, peanut, or pistachio.

12. Mixed nuts and dried or fresh fruit with yogurt.

13. Make smoothies in the blender out of silken tofu, milk, juice or water, fruit, and ground flax seed.

LUNCH OR DINNER FOODS

1. Build your salad around half a cup of beans, adding any combination of: mixed mesclun greens, baby spinach, avocado, fruit, sesame or ground flax seeds, vegetables, nuts, scallions, grated carrots. Now dress it with your favorite dressing.

2. On the weekend, roast any combination of the following vegetables: beets, carrots, eggplant, yellow and green zucchini, winter squash, Brussels sprouts, asparagus, turnips, colored peppers, cauliflower, onion, garlic, sweet potatoes, yams, or green beans. Enjoy roasted vegetables with a simple olive oil and balsamic vinegar dressing, salted and peppered to taste, or topped with another favorite dressing. Add a few cooked beans from the freezer and a sprinkle of toasted sunflower, pumpkin, poppy, sesame or ground flax seeds.

3. Make a quick salad out of cooked chickpeas, sliced tomatoes, cilantro or parsley, lime or lemon juice, ground cumin, salt, pepper, scallions, and avocado.

4. Make a quick soup, adding some tofu, fresh or frozen spinach, garlic, ginger, or any other herbs or spices to a miso-and-water broth.

5. Make another quick soup with V-8 vegetable juice, cooked beans, spices, and herbs.

6. Build a salad using your favorite dressing on a mixture of greens (lettuce, spinach), beans, vegetables, nuts or seeds, and grilled tofu or tempeh.

7. Make grain-based salads: Sprinkle sesame or sunflower seeds, vegetables, herbs, and spices on either cooked millet, barley, quinoa, couscous, bulgur, or rice, and top with your favorite dressing.

8. Add cooked edamame to garden salads.

9. Make a stew – a vegetarian chili, black bean stew, mixed vegetables with beans, spinach-lentil or split pea stew by adding water, herbs and spices.

10. Serve hummus sandwiches with roasted vegetables or a green salad.

11. Make black bean burritos with vegetables on the side.

12. Make soups or casseroles from mixed grains, vegetables, herbs, and spices.

13. Prepare sandwiches with hummus, tempeh or marinated tofu, grilled vegetables or baby greens.

14. Mix grilled vegetables with beans, tofu or tempeh.

15. Serve Mexican beans in tortillas with lettuce and tomato – simple and delicious.

16. Leftovers can always go with vegetables and fruit.

17. Top a baked or steamed potato with beans and salsa.

18. Combine edamame with pesto and serve over rice or any other grain – or add corn to the edamame with pesto and make that a lunch!

19. Serve steamed or microwaved vegetables with hummus or pesto.

20. Make stir-fried cabbage with mung bean sprouts or edamame beans.

21. Make a salad with greens, vegetables, avocado, nuts, edamame or other beans, fruit, or roasted beets.

22. Beans or roasted vegetables are delicious with dry peanut or sesame seed chutney (p. 62).

23. Muthia (p. 113) or upma (p. 107) goes well with a green salad.

24. Roasted vegetables can be served over rice or any grain or bean or in a pita pocket.

25. Pureed roasted vegetables can be used as a sauce over rice and beans.

26. Ground flax or sesame seeds may be sprinkled on just about any food.

DINNER FOODS

You've just returned from work, it's 5:30 p.m., and the whole family is tired and hungry. But – you have anticipated this, and this morning you took some *"instant take-out food"* from the freezer and put it in the refrigerator to thaw gently while you were at work. I often freeze the following, which have been cooked separately: mixed grains, beans, rice, leftovers and one-dish meals, different chutneys, sauces, hummus and pesto so they are handy for *"instant take-out meals."* Here are suggestions:

1. Use any of the quick one-dish meals – variations of the khichadi (p. 94). For feeding health, you want a combination of beans, grains, vegetables, and greens. You want the meal to be colorful as well, so use some herbs, spices, and fruits.

2. To enhance flavors here are some ideas:

    Make a vaghar.

    Add a sour taste with any one citrus – lemon, lime, orange; add the zest too if you like.

    Add any herb.

    Add a spice such as ground-roasted cumin (p. 132), coriander-cumin powder (p. 132), garam masala (p. 133), cilantro chutney (p. 65), or dry sesame or peanut chutney (p. 62, 1st variation).

    Add some garlic or onion.

3. Combine any of the following in any combination with or without yogurt and cook:

    Grain, vegetable, herb

    Grain, vegetable, nuts or seeds, herb

    Grain, beans, vegetable, herb

    Grain, beans, vegetable, nuts or seeds, herb

    Beans, vegetable, herb

    Beans, vegetable, herb, nuts or seeds

    Bean flour, vegetable, herb and spice: e.g. muthia, Puda – savory pancakes

    Bean and grain flour, vegetable, herb and spice: e.g. Muthia (p. 113), Puda (p. 109)

4. Top a cooked grain or potato with a simple tahini, peanut or tomato sauce or with defrosted frozen vegetables, some herbs and cooked beans.

5. Make a salad out of lightly steamed vegetables mixed with tofu cubes, a grain or pasta, and your favorite dressing.

6. Mix tomato sauce, kidney beans, corn, ground cumin, chopped cilantro, and chili powder for a quick stew.

7. Stir-fry vegetables and tofu with rice, barley, pasta or any other grain.

8. Top rice or any other cooked grain with cooked pinto, kidney or black beans, chopped tomatoes, chopped cilantro or parsley or even salsa.

9. Add a tomato-based sauce to puréed beans. This will add texture and richness to a quick low-fat soup, stew or other cooked dish.

10. Try a vegetable stir-fry: vegetables, tofu, tempeh or beans with herbs and spices served over a grain such as rice, millet, barley, corn grits, quinoa or even a baked potato. Mix cold cooked Japanese soba noodles with edamame, shredded carrots, julienned peppers, and seeded cucumber strips and toss with a tasty peanut sesame dressing (p. 63, 1st variation).

11. Serve leftover (or planned) chili from the freezer.

12. Reheat a frozen leftover meal.

13. Fill soft tacos or taco shells with beans and vegetables.

14. Serve a salad with beans, legumes, grain or pasta topped with a marinara sauce.

15. Try khichadi (p. 94) with different combinations: millet and black lentils, rice and split mung beans, quinoa with black lentils.

16. Make a quick stir-fry with frozen bean sprouts or edamame, colored diced sweet peppers from the freezer and fresh red or green cabbage. Dress it with spices or herbs such as cilantro or parsley. Enjoy it over rice, a potato, bread, tortilla or in a pita pocket.

17. Mix grains with pesto, hummus, nut butter or a favorite sauce or dressing, some heated frozen kale or other greens.

18. Stir some pesto or your favorite sauce or dressing into thawed frozen leftover pulses. I enjoy edamame or other beans with pesto.

19. A quick miso soup with tofu or tempeh-add some garlic and greens to the soup.

SNACKS

1. Roasted chick peas with turmeric (p. 74)

2. Fruit, fresh or dried, with a few nuts.

3. Serve vegetables with raita, pesto or hummus.

4. Scoop up bean dip and salsa with baked tortilla chips.

5. Serve air-popped popcorn

6. Eat fruit with plain yogurt.

7. Enjoy cooked or reheated edamame in the pod or shelled, hot or cold.

8. Combine dried fruit, nuts, seeds, and chocolate chips.

9. Serve heated canned or frozen beans with cilantro chutney (p. 65). If you like, add heated frozen corn.

10. An instant soup of V-8 vegetable juice, cooked beans, and roasted vegetables, paired with a green salad with fruit and avocado makes a hearty snack.

11. Top a cooked and halved potato with hummus, pesto, salsa, or grated cheese.

12. Pack celery stalks with nut butter (peanut, sunflower, almond, cashew, etc.) and raisins.

13. Serve crackers with hummus or almond butter or any other nut butter.

14. Pair an apple or banana with peanut butter.

BEVERAGES

1. Serve tea hot or iced: green, black, white, herbal or spiced tea, plain or with milk (dairy or non-dairy).

2. Try adding ground cloves to boiling water or to green, black or white tea.

3. Make mint tea by pouring hot water over fresh or dried mint leaves.

4. For cinnamon tea, add ¼ tsp ground cinnamon to hot water.

5. Cloves and cinnamon in hot water help at the onset of a cold.

6. Make fennel tea by steeping fennel seeds in hot water.

7. Add ¼ tsp ground cardamom to hot water to make a delicious tea.

8. Pour hot water over a lemon or an orange slice and add some zest. Or just use zest in the hot water.

9. Use the recipe for mango lassi, India's famous yogurt drink (p. 129).

10. Try chaash, another Indian yogurt drink (p. 129).

www.FeedingHealth.com

Beverages

Tea Masala
– Chai Masala

Simple

Drinking tea has been linked to several health benefits; these are attributed to its flavonoid content. Adding spices increases the antioxidant content as well as flavor. There are many versions of the chai (tea) masala. Here is what I like and use daily in my hot tea:

INGREDIENTS:

Cardamom ground . . . . 5 T
Ginger ground, dry . . . . 4 T
Cinnamon ground . . . . 1 T
Cloves ground . . . . .1 t
Black pepper ground. . . . . ¼ t
Nutmeg ground . . . . ¼ t

DIRECTIONS:

1. Assemble and prepare all ingredients.

2. Mix all of the above ingredients together and store in a tightly sealed glass jar.

To Make 1 cup of Chai Tea:

INGREDIENTS:

Water . . . . .4 oz
Milk dairy or non-dairy. . . . . .4 oz
Black tea leaves (or black or green tea bag 1) . . . . .1 t
Chai masala . . . . ⅛ t or to taste
Sugar, honey or other sweetener. . . . . to taste

DIRECTIONS:

1. Assemble and prepare all ingredients.

2. Traditional method is to combine water, milk and chai masala; bring to a boil.

3. Add tea leaves or tea bag, turn heat off; steep tea for 3 to 5 minutes; strain tea.

4. Add sugar, honey or any other sweetener.

5. Enjoy this hot or cold. Traditionally it is enjoyed as a hot beverage.

6. Here is how I enjoy my hot tea every day. I add boiling water to the tea leaves and allow them to steep for 5 minutes. I strain the tea, add the chai masala and a little milk – and it is ready to drink.

VARIATIONS & OPTIONS:

- You can make different versions of this masala mixture depending on your preference and availability of ingredients in your kitchen.

- Omit the black pepper.

- Omit both black pepper and nutmeg.

- Increase the ginger by 1 to 2 T.

- Add ½ to 1 t crushed saffron threads (my favorite) to the recipe.

Mango Lassi

Simple – Serves 2

INGREDIENTS:

Mango pulp. . . . . 2 Cups canned or 2 very ripe fresh mangoes

Yogurt low fat, dairy or non-dairy, plain. . . . . .1 ½ Cups

Honey . . . . .2 t

DIRECTIONS:

1. Assemble and prepare all ingredients.

2. If using fresh mangoes, wash, peel and cut the mangoes.

3. Blend all three ingredients in a blender and pour over ice in tall glasses.

Darshana's Chaash

Simple – Serves 4

This yogurt drink is the beverage of choice with meals in south India. This is from my niece Darshana.

INGREDIENTS:

Yogurt low fat, dairy or non-dairy, plain. . . . . .2 Cups

Cold water . . . . .2 Cups

Salt . . . . ⅛ t or to taste

Cumin ground . . . . ½ t

Asafetida (hing) . . . . pinch

DIRECTIONS:

1. Assemble and prepare all ingredients.

2. Beat yogurt with salt, cumin and asafetida.

3. Add water and beat to mix with yogurt.

4. Serve in tall glasses over ice.

Masalas

Roasted Cumin Seeds, Ground

Simple

Cumin seeds may stimulate the secretion of pancreatic enzymes necessary for proper digestion and nutrient assimilation. They are an excellent source of iron, an integral part of hemoglobin, which transports oxygen from the lungs to all cells.[8,9,12] Dry-roasting the cumin seeds before grinding them enhances the aroma and the flavor.

INGREDIENTS:

Cumin seeds. . . . . ¼ Cup

DIRECTIONS:

1. Dry-roast cumin seeds in a small heavy-bottomed skillet on medium-high heat until they turn a few shades darker and give off their delicious roasted aroma.

2. Transfer roasted cumin to a plate for cooling.

3. Grind the cooled seeds in a coffee mill or spice grinder.

4. Store in an airtight glass jar.

5. Sprinkle this on yogurt, cucumbers, tomatoes, grains, beans or legumes. Once you start using roasted ground cumin seeds you will want to keep some in your spice rack.

6. In the same grinder you can now make coriander-cumin powder.

Coriander-Cumin Powder

Coriander seeds contain a variety of phytonutrients. They are a very good source of fiber and a good source of iron, magnesium and manganese. Cumin seeds provide manganese and iron.[8,9]

INGREDIENTS:

Coriander seeds. . . . . 1 Cup
Cumin seeds. . . . . ⅓ Cup

DIRECTIONS:

1. Separately, dry-roast coriander and cumin seeds in pre-heated heavy-bottomed skillet.

2. Transfer to a plate for cooling.

3. Grind both seeds together to a coarse powder.

4. Store in a glass jar with a tight fitting lid.

5. This powder can be added to just about any vegetable, grain or bean after cooking. For curries, some rice dishes and daals it can be added during the cooking process.

6. In the same grinder you can now make garam masala.

Garam Masala
Simple

Herbs and spices, in use since approximately 5,000 B.C.E., are among the richest sources of antioxidants and play a central role in Indian cooking. They can reduce salt, fat and sugar by adding flavor to foods without adding unwanted sodium and fat calories.

INGREDIENTS:

Cumin seeds. . . . . .1 t
Cloves. . . . . .1 t
Black peppercorns. . . . . .1 t
Hot red chili peppers dried, whole. .2
Coriander seeds. . . . . 1 T
Bay leaves 2
Cinnamon . . . . 1 3" long stick (or 2 t ground)
Cardamom seeds. . . . . .2 t
Nutmeg grated . . . . ¼ t
Turmeric. . . . . .1 t

DIRECTIONS:

1. Assemble and prepare all ingredients.

2. Separately, in a preheated heavy-bottomed skillet, over medium heat, dry roast cumin seeds, cloves, peppercorns, hot red chili peppers and coriander seeds. Roast separately and very lightly the cinnamon stick and bay leaves. Do not roast cardamom seeds, nutmeg or turmeric.

3. Add cardamom seeds to the warm roasted spices. Allow cooling.

4. Grind the cooled roasted spices together into a powder. Add nutmeg and turmeric (plus ground cinnamon, if using) and store in a glass jar with a tight fitting lid.

5. Garam masala can be used to flavor any bean, grain or vegetable dish.

6. You may want to triple the recipe so you have plenty of garam masala ready to use.

In the same grinder you can now make Sāmbhar masala.

Sāmbhar Masala

Simple

There are many variations of Sāmbhar masala used in South Indian dishes. This masala is added to lentil daals served with rice, idli or dosa. Add this masala to any puréed beans to make a quick daal or add it to steamed vegetables or even grains.

INGREDIENTS:

Cumin seeds	2 t
Fenugreek seeds	2 t
Hot red chili peppers dry whole	to taste or 3 to 4
Black peppercorns	1 t
Coriander seeds	¼ Cup
Oil	1 t
Channa daal or **yellow split peas**	¼ Cup
Turmeric	1 t
Asafetida (hing)	⅛ t
Salt	to taste or ¼ t

DIRECTIONS:

1. Assemble and prepare all ingredients.

2. Preheat a heavy-bottomed skillet over medium heat and roast – separately – cumin seeds, fenugreek seeds, whole red chili peppers, peppercorns and coriander seeds. Allow cooling.

3. Sauté channa daal in oil for 2 to 3 minutes. Allow cooling.

4. When cooled, grind all the roasted ingredients to a powder.

5. Add salt, asafetida and turmeric; mix well.

6. Store in a tightly sealed glass jar.

Masala Mix for Vegetables & Beans

Simple

VARIATIONS & OPTIONS:

- Substitute fresh or dry unsweetened grated coconut for peanuts.

- Substitute any other nuts or seeds for peanuts.

- Substitute soy or mung bean flour for chickpea flour. However, chickpea flour has a very pleasant sweet taste and aroma, which is very different from the aroma of soy flour.

- Add 2 T ground flax seeds when mixing the ingredients together.

Optional ingredients to add to this masala mix at time of cooking:

- **Garlic** minced

- **Ginger** fresh or frozen grated

- **Garam masala** to taste

- **Oil** to mix with masala and vegetables or beans

- **Lemon** or **lime,** juiced, to taste

- **Cilantro** with tender stems, chopped

INGREDIENTS:

Sesame seeds	¼ Cup
Chickpea flour (besan)	¼ Cup
Peanuts chopped	¼ Cup
Coriander-cumin powder	¼ Cup
Red chili pepper (or Cayenne to taste)	2 t
Turmeric	1 t
Salt	to taste or ½ t
Asafetida (hing)	pinch

DIRECTIONS:

1. Prepare and assemble all ingredients.

2. Preheat a heavy-bottomed skillet over medium heat and roast – separately – sesame seeds first then with heat off roast the chickpea flour to prevent burning the flour.

3. Mix all of the above ingredients together, use what you need right away and/or store unused masala in a glass jar with a tight-fitting lid.

4. Add this masala mixture to okra, eggplant, colored peppers, zucchini, cauliflower, potatoes and onions or any combination of these vegetables. Add this masala when the vegetables or beans are half cooked.

5. Make extra and store in the refrigerator or freezer for future use. I always keep some in the freezer ready for using.

6. Use this masala mix on grilled or roasted vegetables with chopped cilantro and lemon or limejuice:

    Grill vegetables with a coating of oil and minced garlic.

    Add spice mixture to hot grilled vegetables, stir to mix, top with cilantro and lemon or limejuice and allow to rest covered for 5 minutes before serving. Do not add masala mix to vegetables on the grill – the flour and spices will burn.

Vaghar combinations for ajwain seeds in oil:

1. Ajwain seeds
2. Ajwain seeds with mustard seeds
3. Ajwain seeds and garlic

Vaghar combinations for black mustard seeds in oil:

1. Black mustard seeds and hing
2. Black mustard seeds, onion and hing
3. Black mustard seeds and ajwain seeds
4. Black mustard seeds, cumin seeds and hing
5. Black mustard seeds, cumin seeds, onion and hing
6. Black mustard seeds, fenugreek seeds and hing
7. Black mustard seeds, cumin seeds, fenugreek seeds and hing
8. Black mustard seeds with sesame seeds and hing

Vaghar combinations for cumin seeds in oil:

1. Cumin seeds and hing
2. Cumin seeds, mustard seeds and hing
3. Cumin seeds, fenugreek seeds and hing
4. Cumin seeds, ginger, garlic and hing

Vaghar with cinnamon stick in oil, butter or ghee:

1. Cinnamon stick
2. Cinnamon stick and cloves
3. Cinnamon stick, cloves and bay leaf
4. Cinnamon stick, cloves and cardamom seeds
5. Cinnamon stick, cloves, cumin seeds and bay leaf

Vaghar with cloves in oil, butter or ghee:

1. Cloves
2. Cloves with hing
3. Cloves with black mustard seed
4. Cloves with cinnamon stick, cumin, black mustard seeds and hing

Vaghar with fenugreek seeds in oil:

1. Fenugreek seeds and hing
2. Fenugreek seeds, cumin seeds and hing
3. Fenugreek seeds, mustard seeds, onion and hing
4. Fenugreek seeds, cumin seeds, mustard seeds and hing
5. Fenugreek seeds, onion and hing

Vaghar with garlic in oil or ghee:

1. Garlic
2. Garlic and ginger
3. Garlic, ginger and onion
4. Garlic, ginger, onion and hot green chili

Vaghar with ginger in oil:

1. Ginger sautéed
2. Ginger and onion sautéed

Vaghar with Limbdo (curry leaves) in oil:

1. Limbdo with black mustard seeds and hing
2. Limbdo with black mustard seeds, urad daal and hing

Vaghar with Sesame seeds in oil:

1. Sesame seeds and hing
2. Sesame seeds, cumin and hing
3. Sesame seeds, mustard seeds and hing
4. Sesame seeds, cumin and garlic
5. Sesame seeds, garlic and ginger
6. Sesame seeds, cumin seeds, garlic and ginger

Vaghar with either urad or channa daal in oil:

1. Channa or Urad daal with hing
2. Channa or Urad daal with limbdo leaves and hing
3. Channa or Urad daal with black mustard seeds and hing
4. Channa or Urad daal with limbdo leaves, hing and black mustard seeds

Section 3: Menus & Entrées

Menus:

Beets sweet and sour (p. 23)
Snow peas with garlic and ginger (p. 33)
Quinoa with edamame (p. 92)
Raita with coconut and cilantro (p. 56)
    Calories: 388 **Protein:** 17 g **Total carbohydrate:** 50 g

Cabbage Stir-fried – Salad (p. 19)
Barley and mung beans khichadi (p. 96)
Raita with Mushrooms (p. 54)
    Calories: 403 **Protein:** 17 g **Total carbohydrate:** 57 g

Cauliflower (p. 21)
Khichadi (p. 94)
Summer squash (p. 27)
Kadhi (p. 59)
    Calories: 427 **Protein:** 17 g **Total carbohydrate:** 59 g

Spinach stir-fry (p. 24)
Raita with radish (p. 50)
Edamame with stir fried vegetables (p. 18)
Quinoa (p. 91)
    Calories: 383 **Protein:** 16 g **Total carbohydrate:** 53 g

Mixed vegetable salad (p. 47)
Mixed Vegetables (Undhiyu) (p. 28)
Gujarati mung beans daal (p. 77)
Oat flour roti (p. 105)
    Calories: 422 **Protein:** 17 g **Total carbohydrate:** 63 g

Stir-fried hot cereal (p. 101)
Raita with cucumber (p. 52)
Dill with split mung beans (p. 22)
Okra stir-fried (p. 38)
    Calories: 417 **Protein:** 16 g **Total carbohydrate:** 55 g

Gujarati tuver daal (split pigeon peas daal) (p. 78)
Brown basmati rice (p. 87)
Peas with tofu (p. 34)
Cabbage Salad, Green and Red (p. 44)
    Calories: 567 **Protein:** 20 g **Total carbohydrate:** 74 g

Mung bean sprouts salad (p. 75)
Raita with banana (p. 51)
Pinto beans (p. 80)
Oat flour roti (p. 105)
    Calories: 381 **Protein:** 16 g **Total carbohydrate:** 57 g

Quinoa (p. 91)
Dry green pea ragdo – dry green pea curry (p.76)
Carrots stir-fried with sprouts and vegetables (p. 20)
Mixed vegetable salad (p. 47)
   Calories: 480 **Protein:** 18 g **Total carbohydrate:** 70 g

Asparagus khichadi (p. 95)
Broccoli (p. 39)
Eggplant – simple (p. 29)
Raita with coconut and cilantro (p. 56)
   Calories: 414 **Protein:** 16 g **Total carbohydrate:** 59 g

Sundal (p. 79)
Quinoa (p.91)
Garlic in yogurt (p. 58)
Carrots stir-fried with sprouts and vegetables (p. 20)
   Calories: 448 **Protein:** 19 g **Total carbohydrate:** 61 g

Lentil sprouts and rice khichadi (p. 97)
Asparagus (p. 40)
Snow peas with garlic and ginger (p. 33)
Raita with cucumber (p. 52)
   Calories: 416 **Protein:** 18 g **Total carbohydrate:** 59 g

Entrées

Quinoa with edamame (p. 92)
   Calories: 181 **Protein:** 7 g **Carbohydrate:** 27 g

Rice with cabbage and peas (p.88)
   Calories: 206 **Protein:** 5.5 g **Carbohydrate:** 34 g

Barley and baby crimini mushrooms (p. 89)
   Calories: 202 **Protein:** 6g **Carbohydrate:** 32 g

Asparagus khichadi (p. 95)
   Calories: 207 **Protein:** 7 g **Carbohydrate:** 38 g

Barley and mung beans khichadi (p. 96)
   Calories: 217 **Protein:** 9 g **Carbohydrate:** 37 g

Lentil sprouts khichadi (p. 97)
   Calories: 203 **Protein:** 7 g **Carbohydrate:** 36 g

Muthia (p. 113)
   Calories: 198 **Protein:** 6 g **Carbohydrate:** 26 g

Rice with beans and vegetables (p. 98)
   Calories: 269 **Protein:** 9 g **Carbohydrate:** 41 g

Chickpea stew (p. 118)
   Calories: 247 **Protein:** 10 g **Carbohydrate:** 39 g

Health Benefits
of Herbs and Spices

Herbs and spices, in use since approximately 5,000 B.C.E., are among the richest sources of antioxidants, and play a central role in Indian cooking. They can reduce salt, fat and sugar by adding flavor to foods without adding unwanted sodium and fat calories. Herbs are from the leaf, while spices are derived from any other part of the plant, like buds (e.g., cloves), bark (e.g., cinnamon), roots (e.g., ginger), berries (e.g., peppercorns) and aromatic seeds (e.g., cumin).

The ORAC (Oxygen Radical Absorbance Capacity) analysis measures the antioxidant capacity of foods. The more free radicals a food can absorb and deactivate, the higher the ORAC score. Researchers suggest we consume 3,000 to 5,000 ORAC units a day, but most of us average only 1,200. Many herbs and spices, such as cinnamon, cloves, coriander, dill, garlic, ginger, mustard seeds, turmeric, garlic and many others have high ORAC scores.

Some common herbs and spices used in Indian cooking are hing (asafetida), ajwain seeds, bay leaves, black pepper, cardamom, red chili peppers, cinnamon, cloves, coriander, cumin, dill, fenugreek, ginger, mustard, nutmeg, turmeric and dried leaves from the neem tree – called curry leaves. Below are the health benefits of some common herbs and spices used in Indian cooking, relating to blood sugars, cholesterol and high blood pressure. Some of these spices have medicinal properties and thus should not be consumed in quantities greater than used in normal cooking if taken along with prescription medications. Bitter melon, onions and garlic are used frequently in Indian cooking and also have medicinal qualities.

Ajwain (Bishop's weed) seeds look almost like celery seeds. They are available in South Asian grocery stores, or can be ordered by mail. Substitute oregano or thyme if you do not have ajwain seeds. They contain khellin, which increases levels of high-density lipoprotein (HDL- the good cholesterol) without affecting total cholesterol or triglycerides.

Bitter Melon resembles a light green, pointed cucumber and is used as a vegetable or is pickled. It is occasionally dried. Bitter melon fruit and seeds have been shown to improve glucose tolerance and reduce blood sugar in individuals with type 2 diabetes. Pregnant women should avoid bitter melon. Individuals with diabetes should eat bitter melon cautiously if they are taking blood sugar lowering drugs, as there is a report of additive blood sugar lowering effect in a patient taking Diabinese and eating large quantities of bitter melon curry.

Chili peppers contain a substance called capsaicin. The hotter the chili pepper, the more capsaicin it contains. Red chili peppers are shown to reduce blood cholesterol, triglyceride levels, and platelet aggregation.

Cinnamon (only Cassia) has been shown to have an effect on blood sugar in humans. However, Cinnamomum verum also contains the ingredient thought to be responsible for lowering blood sugar. Individuals on medications for diabetes should monitor blood sugar closely if consuming large quantities of cinnamon.

142   www.FeedingHealth.com

Cloves have a variety of phytonutrients and contain a volatile oil that can consist of up to 90% eugenol, which inhibits platelet activity and functions as an anti-inflammatory.

Coriander has been shown to lower blood sugar in animals. In parts of India it has traditionally been used as an anti-inflammatory agent. Coriander's exceptional phytonutrient content, flavonoids and active phenolic acid compounds contribute to its healing properties. According to Ayurveda, coriander is cooling and aids digestion.

Cumin seeds and powder may have hypoglycemic effects. According to Ayurveda, cumin seeds aid digestion and balance all three doshas.

Fenugreek seed powder is taken by pregnant and lactating women in India in the form of a sweet. Fenugreek seeds are used as a cooking spice and are sprouted for cooking with beans; the leaves are eaten as a fresh green vegetable. Fenugreek improves insulin sensitivity in individuals with type 1 and type 2 diabetes and has been used to treat diabetes, constipation and hyperlipidemia.

Ginger contains anti-inflammatory compounds called gingerols. Taking large quantities of ginger along with diabetes medications might cause a drop in blood sugar. Ginger may reduce blood pressure in a way similar to some blood pressure and heart disease medications. Avoid taking large supplemental quantities (more than used in normal everyday cooking) of ginger if also taking medications for blood pressure and diabetes.

Mustard seeds and powder, like other Brassicas, contains plenty of phytonutrients. Isothiocyanates in mustard seed and other Brassicas have been repeatedly studied for their anti-cancer effects.

Turmeric has been used in Chinese and Indian medicine as an anti-inflammatory agent. Curcumin, the active ingredient in turmeric, has anti-inflammatory effects. Turmeric might slow blood clotting, so taking large quantities along with medications that also slow clotting might increase chances of bruising and bleeding.

Onion may help reduce cholesterol levels and blood pressure; show hypoglycemic actions and diuretic effects and inhibit platelet aggregation. Onion's antioxidants, such as quercetin, provide anti-inflammatory benefits.

Garlic's active ingredients allicin and allyl propyl disulphide are hypoglycemic and have been shown to improve blood sugar control. Researchers have noted an association between garlic use and increased serum insulin and improved liver glycogen storage. Garlic has been used to improve many conditions related to the heart and blood system, including high blood pressure, high cholesterol, coronary heart disease, heart attack, and hardening of the arteries.

Cinnamon, fenugreek seeds, garlic, onion, ginger, cumin, coriander and bitter melon are examples of spices and foods used frequently in Indian cooking which have a beneficial effect on blood sugar. However, it is important to be aware of the cumulative effects of these spices when consumed in quantities greater than used in normal cooking while taking medications to reduce blood sugar. For this reason, individuals with diabetes need to monitor blood sugars carefully. As we can see, many of these ingredients, if used daily, could have a cumulative, beneficial effect on our health.

Sprouting Beans, Grains, or Seeds

Sprouts have long been enjoyed in Asian cuisines for their crunchiness, fresh and delicate flavor, and nutritional value. For the past decade or more, they have been found at American salad bars and in the produce section of supermarkets, so more people are using them. Familiar sprouts are alfalfa and mung bean, but you may also see lentil, soybean, buckwheat, Chinese cabbage, watercress, radish, sunflower, and mustard sprouts in grocery stores. They are a low-calorie addition to salads and meals and will increase nutrient intake, especially during the winter months.

Growing sprouts is easy. Almost any seed or bean can be sprouted – but make sure the ones you select are intended for eating because seeds for planting are often treated with fungicides.

1. Rinse ⅓ cup beans, grains, or seeds thoroughly and place them in a clean quart-size glass jar. Fill the jar ¾ full with warm water. Cover the mouth of the jar with cheesecloth and secure with a rubber band. Soak (unrefrigerated) overnight or up to 20 hours. Smaller seeds take shorter soaking times (6-8 hours). Do not over soak as the seeds could ferment.

2. Drain the soaked beans, grains, or seeds and rinse with fresh water. Drain again and place the jar on its side in a warm dark draft-free place. An unheated oven, cabinet or even in a container on top of your refrigerator will work.

3. Rinse and drain once or twice each day, returning the jar to its dark draft-free place after each rinsing. Sprouting times vary depending on the size of the bean, grain, or seed, but most are ready in 2-3 days. To turn the sprouts green, place them in indirect sunlight on the last growing day.

Here is another method I use exclusively because it allows me to sprout up to 2 cups of dry mung beans at a time: Use a large colander instead of a jar. Rinse 1/3 cup to 2 cups beans, grains, or seeds thoroughly in a bowl. Soak in 3 cups of water overnight or up to 20 hours. I usually keep the bowl on my kitchen counter next to the sink for convenience. Drain the soaked beans, grains, or seeds and rinse with fresh water. Drain again and put them in the strainer or colander. Place this in a larger bowl, cover the bowl, and place in a dark draft free place. Now follow the same steps described above.

Food For Thought!

Imagine sitting down to a well-deserved meal. Your plate is filled with an assortment of colorful vegetables, grains and beans. The exotic aroma of fresh spices beckons, and as you begin to eat, you are happily aware of the contrasting sensation of crisp vegetables mingling with the grainy-textured quinoa or rice and legumes. Your meal is colorful, high in nutrients, low in fat and absolutely delicious! This is the essence of feeding health.

Enjoy these foods and spices with the knowledge that they can bring positive changes to your health. Serve them with love to your family and friends. May this book inspire you to embrace a healthier lifestyle, beginning in the kitchen. And now, my readers, **Prem thee jamjo!** – which means, "Please eat with love and passion!"

To eat is a necessity, but to eat intelligently is an art.
– La Rochefoucauld, 1665

Glossary

Ajwain seeds look almost like celery seeds. They are available in Indian grocery stores or ordered by mail. Substitute oregano or thyme if you do not have ajwain seeds.

Asafetida (also known as **hing**) is a resin with a strong aroma and is available in Indian grocery stores. Although used in very small quantities it imparts a flavor to the food.

Black mustard seeds are available in Indian grocery stores. Grind the seeds in a spice grinder to a coarse powder.

Chapatti flour is a very finely ground whole-wheat flour sold in Indian grocery stores or ordered by mail.

Chickpea flour is also known as besan or gram flour and is available in Indian grocery stores or ordered by mail. I suggest storing it in the refrigerator or freezer.

Cilantro, fresh green coriander, is a very popular herb in India. It is easily available in most grocery stores. Parsley may be substituted for cilantro.

Coriander seeds are the seeds of the coriander plant. They are used in their ground form in Indian cooking.

Cumin seeds, shaped like caraway seeds, are used whole and ground in Indian cooking. They are easily available in most grocery stores.

Curry leaves are very aromatic when fresh and are available in Indian grocery stores. They are sold fresh and dried. Refrigerate or freeze fresh curry leaves.

Fenugreek seeds are a dull yellow color and are also available in grocery stores.

Ghee is clarified butter; no milk solids and moisture remain in the clarified butter. All Indian grocers sell it. Although ayurveda promotes ghee, it is important to note that ghee contains saturated fat and if you choose to use ghee consume it in moderation.

Gluten is a protein found in wheat, rye and barley; it is not found in oats. However, if oats are processed alongside wheat products, they may be "contaminated" with gluten. Based on Dr. Fasano's research 1% of the population may have celiac disease and non-celiac gluten sensitivity may affect 6% of the population. Individuals with celiac disease or with non-celiac gluten sensitivity are unable to eat foods containing gluten.

References

1. Prior, Ronald L, A Daily Dose of Antioxidants? Agricultural Research/March 2008, 4-5, USDA

2. Heber, David M.D. Ph.D., Bowerman, Susan M.S. R.D. What color is your diet? Regan Books, Harper Collins, New York, 2001

3. Phytonutrient information
www.ars.usda.gov/Aboutus/docs.htm?docid=4142

4. www.cnpp.usda.gov/DGAs2010-DGACReport.htm

5. Jones, David S, M.D. Textbook of Functional Medicine, Institute for Functional Medicine, Gig Harbor, WA, 2006

6. Bliss, Rosalie Marion, Dawson-Hughes, Bess, Agricultural Research, USDA, Nov/Dec 2009, pg 20

7. www.eatright.org

8. Sheldon Margen, M.D., and the Editors of the University of California at Berkley Wellness Letter, The Wellness Encyclopedia of Food and Nutrition. New York, Rebus, Distributed by Random House, 1992

9. George Mateljan, the world's healthiest foods, Essential Guide for the healthiest way of eating. GMF Publishing, 2007.

10. USDA – www.nal.usda.gov/fnic/foodcomp/search/

11. Furnishing the Facts on Fiber, Fiber Fact Sheet
www.resistantstarch.com/ResistantStarch/Home/

12. Amadea Morningstar, Urmila Desai, The Ayurvedic Cookbook, A Personalized guide to Good Nutrition and Health. Lotus Light Press, 1991.

13. www.glycemicindex.com
Most comprehensive resource for glycemic index food lists.

14. Natural Medicines Comprehensive Database –
http://naturaldatabase.therapeuticresearch.com:80/home.aspx?cs=CEPDA~MBR&s=ND

15. Brighenti F, Benini L, Del Rio D, et al. Colonic fermentation of indigestible carbohydrates contributes to the second-meal effect. Am J Clin Nutr. 2006;83:817-822.

16. Environmental Working Group – www.ewg.org

Herbs & Spice References

1. Natural Medicines Comprehensive Database http://naturaldatabase.therapeuticresearch. com:80/home.aspx?cs=CEPDA~MBR&s=ND. 2011. Accessed May 11, 2011.

2. Harvengt C, Desager JP. HDL-cholesterol increase in normolipaemic subjects on khellin: a pilot study. *Int J Clin Pharmacol Res.*1983;3:363-6.

3. Morningstar A, Desai U. *The Ayurvedic Cookbook, A Personalized Guide to Good Nutrition and Health.* Twin Lakes, WI: Lotus Light Press; 1991.

4. Heck AM, DeWitt BA, Lukes AL. Potential interactions between alternative therapies and warfarin. *Am J Health Syst Pharm.* 2000;57(13):1221-7.

5. Leung L, Birtwhistle R, Kotecha J, Hannah S, Cuthbertson S. Anti-diabetic and hypoglycaemic effects of Momordica charantia (bitter melon): a mini review. *Br J Nutr.* 2009;102(12):1703-8.

6. Krawinkel MB, Keding GB. Bitter gourd (Momordica Charantia): A dietary approach to hyperglycemia. *Nutr Rev.* 2006;64:331-7.

7. Tani Y, Fuijoka T, Sumioka M, Furichi Y, Hamada H, Watanabe T. Effects of capsinoid on serum and liver lipids in hyperlipidemic rats. *J Nutr Sci Vitaminol* (Tokyo). 2004; 50:351–355.

8. Raghavendra RH, Naidu KA. Spice active principles as the inhibitors of human platelet aggregation and thromboxane biosynthesis. *Prostaglandins Leukot Essent Fatty Acids.* 2009;81(1):73-8.

9. Dhanapakiam P, Joseph JM, Ramaswamy VK, Moorthi M, Kumar AS. The cholesterol lowering property of coriander seeds (Coriandrum sativum): mechanism of action. *J Environ Biol.* 2008;29 (1):53-6.

10. National Center for Complementary and Alternative Medicine. Fenugreek. http://nccam.nih. gov/health/fenugreek/. Published March 2007. Updated July 2010. Accessed May 2011.

11. Izzo AA, Di Carlo G, Borrelli F, Ernst E. Cardiovascular pharmacotherapy and herbal medicines: the risk of drug interaction. *Int J Cardiol.* 2005;98(1):1-14.

12. Liu CT, Sheen LY, Lii CK. Does garlic have a role as an antidiabetic agent? *Mol Nutr Food Res.* 2007;51(11):1353-64.

13. Rahman K, Lowe GM. Garlic and cardiovascular disease: a critical review. *J Nutr.* 2006;136(3 Suppl):736S-740S.

14. Srivastava KC. Effect of onion and ginger consumption on platelet thromboxane production in humans. *Prostaglandins Leukot Essent Fatty Acids.* 1989;35:183-5.

15. Thomson M, Al-Qattan KK, Al-Sawan SM, The use of ginger (Zingiber officinale Rosc.) as a potential anti-inflammatory and antithrombotic agent. *Prostaglandins Leukot Essent Fatty Acids.* 2002;67:475-8.

16. United States Food and Drug Administration (FDA). Database of Select Committee on GRAS Substances (SCOGS) Reviews. http://www.accessdata.fda.gov/scripts/fcn/fcnNavigation. cfm?rpt=scogsListing. Updated Oct. 31, 2006. Accessed May 16, 2011.

17. Srinivasan K. Plant foods in the management of diabetes mellitus: spices as beneficial antidiabetic food adjuncts. *Int J Food Sci Nutr.* 2005;56(6):399-414.

18. Ali M, Thomson M, Afzal M. Garlic and onions: their effect on eicosanoid metabolism and its clinical relevance. *Prostaglandins Leukot Essent Fatty Acids.* 2000;62(2):55-73.

Index

Notes

CPSIA information can be obtained at www.ICGtesting.com
Printed in the USA
LVOW112124080312

272294LV00002B/380/P

9 780983 525806